Uncovering
the
Wisdom
of the
Heartmind

Uncovering the Wisdom of the Heartmind

"Shaking Down Seed"

and

Other Stories of Ordinary Goodness

Lin Jensen

A publication supported by
THE KERN FOUNDATION

Quest Books
Theosophical Publishing House

Wheaton, Illinois ♦ Chennai (Madras), India

The Theosophical Publishing House
P. O. Box 270
Wheaton, IL 60189-0270

A publication of the Theosophical Publishing House,
a department of the Theosophical Society in America

The character for *Heartmind* featured in this book was brushed
by Weikun Cheng, Professor of Chinese History,
California State University at Chico.

Library of Congress Cataloging-in-Publication Data

Jensen, Lin.
    Uncovering the wisdom of the heartmind: "shaking down
seed" and other stories of ordinary goodness / Lin Jensen.
        p.   cm.
ISBN 0-8356-0775-5
    1. Spiritual life—Zen buddhism.   2. Compassion
(Buddhism)   I. Title
BQ9286.2.J46   1999
294.3'4432—dc21   99-12376
                                                                    CIP

    4   3   2   1   *   99   00   01   02   03   04   05
Printed in the United States of America

To Father,
who taught me to endure,

and to Karen,
who taught me to belong.

CONTENTS

OUR ONLY NAME

GATHERING

VOICES

GOING BEYOND

*"I have asked to know
The wisdom of the Heartmind
That I may help all living things."*

PREFACE

"Shaking Down Seed," the first essay of this collection, seems to me so obvious and simple that it reads like a child's tale. Yet once having written it, I have been unable to outgrow it. The central action of the essay consists of shaking seed loose from a frozen bird feeder so that the winter birds can eat. There's little more to it than that—just the simple image of an act as plain and ordinary as washing dishes.

But that's the point, you see. I wash dishes about as regularly and often as I do any other single thing. And when I'm not washing dishes, I'm likely to be doing something else that is equally ordinary. To outgrow such things would be to outgrow my life, which is only what is right in front of me—the plain fact of being here. It's not possible to locate myself in any other place.

No matter how simple an act, whatever it might be, it holds within it the whole of our lives. We discover ourselves less in thought than in action. It is what we do that tells. Every ordinary act is, in that way, a metaphor. In the act that shakes loose the seed, we intuit the whole of the thing and know our situation from the center outward.

If I have written well, you will find nothing outside

yourself in these pages, which are best approached as you would approach a mirror, expecting your own face to appear. The abbess of a Buddhist monastery, whose legs are paralyzed by diabetes, announces in perfect cheerfulness that she is "dying from the bottom up." In her words, infirmity itself gathers voice to strengthen us, so that we take courage as from our own speaking. The entire population of horned larks, vast flocks numbering in the thousands, suddenly and inexplicably vanishes from a mountain valley in northeastern California, and in that void each of us enters the stilled and silenced field of his own absence. A fawn, struck down on a country road, cries out in the very instant of its dying, and innocence everywhere echoes that cry. In perfect tenderness, a son bathes the soiled body of a dying father, and all of us are cleansed by the act.

If you allow your mind to enter these pages unprepared and unguarded, you rely on intuition, which is direct knowing. Intuition requires that we trust ourselves to know more than we think we know. In Buddhism, we refer to the source of this intuitive knowing as the Heartmind, which we understand to be our own true mind that resides within all consciousness and is the source of a natural and inherent wisdom. The Heartmind answers its own call: it is truth recognizing truth, love discovering love, hate confirming hate, sorrow answering sorrow, joy receiving joy. In our human quest for understanding, we acquire nothing that is not already ours. We can trust wisdom to know itself on sight.

Heartmind is a particularly appropriate word for naming a wisdom comprised not of intellectual achievement and erudition, but of charity, tenderness, benevolence, and sympathy; a wisdom we Buddhists view as the highest intelligence. This compassionate wisdom is less sentiment than act, having little to do with cultivating attitudes of kindliness and everything to do with intuiting what needs to be done. It is the hand that shakes down seed. The abiding effort of a Buddhist is to uncover this wisdom within herself, that she may do good and cease from actions that bring harm and suffering to the world.

It is with this intent that I have written these essays, not for literary ambition but because the book might do some good, some shaking down somewhere. Suffering might be eased a little, a degree of harm averted, encouragement received, the wisdom of the Heartmind uncovered.

HOMAGE

*"I am but earth
tending earth."*

SHAKING DOWN
SEED

At a recent stay in a Buddhist monastery outside Shasta, California, I happened to learn of a practice the monks kept while traveling by car. Whenever they saw the remains of a road kill (some squirrel or deer or raccoon, some dog or cat or magpie or hawk all scattered, torn, or crushed along the swift margins of pavement), all but the driver would raise their hands, palm to palm before bowed heads, and intone a brief memorial to the slain animal. When circumstances permitted, the monks sometimes stopped and performed a short roadside burial and service. "In doing so," they told me, "you pay homage to the source of life."

"It is not possible for us humans to live without doing some harm to others," the monks at Shasta explained. "This is a sorrow, yet a fact." But at the same time, they were concerned to point out to me that in traveling by car one can reduce the degree of harm by slowing down or braking or swerving to avoid collision wherever possible. No one, they told me, could drive the agricultural roads of California's Central Valley in spring or summer without killing insects, whose sudden and violent deaths accumulate in splatters on the windshield. "But we have learned that if you drive slowly in these areas, it is possible to kill far fewer. And when we stop, we can say a brief memorial for the ones we have killed."

At the end of a week I left the monastery and drove home. I had not gone thirty miles when, along a stretch of road lined with deep woods, I came upon a smear of fur and raw flesh stamped onto the pavement by the continual passing of automobile tires. Flung over against a cutbank nearby was the crumpled blackness of a raven that had been drawn to feed on what had been killed trying to cross the road. I was alone in the car but in my mind's eye I saw the monks from Shasta press their hands together and bow to the two lives that had ended there.

My thought goes back to a brief incident of this past winter. It was early morning, a dark half-light at best, and quite cold. I awoke to find that my wife, Karen, had already left the bed. Getting up myself, I found the living room warming from a fire Karen had started in the stove, but she herself was nowhere in the house. And then I saw her from the living room window. She was bundled up in a parka with a hood, and she wore gloves and snow boots that irregularly broke through the frozen crust of the snow as she walked, causing her to sink suddenly and struggle to keep her balance.

I saw then where she was headed in all that frozen darkness. She was making her way to the seed feeder we had set out for the winter birds. The seed on the platform and in the feeder tubes was covered over and frozen, and she was concerned that the wakening birds would be deprived of a food source they had come to depend on. It was a simple act, just a natural sympathy that had risen in her, some sense of responsibility she felt for having raised expectations in a flock of thirty or so juncos.

At the feeder, she scraped stiff snow off the platform. Then she took each of the two feeder tubes in hand and shook them until seed fell down to where the birds could get to it. How sensible and ordinary an act. And yet, in that shaking there, something shook down in me, settled, and was taken up again in nourishment throughout the whole of that winter day and, as you can see, still feeds me now.

My eighty-four-year-old mother called me recently on the phone. She was widowed this past winter and she said to me, "You know, Son, I have never before lived alone." But then, without pausing on that salient fact, she launched into the latest episodes involving Mike, an aging dog she and my father had shared their lives with for many years. She was most interested in telling me about the relationship Mike had established with Charlie, a yearling cat brought by a loving daughter to soothe a mother's grief. And apparently Charlie had done the trick, for here was our mother telling me not only how much Charlie cheered her up, but how his kittenish antics had finally coaxed Mike off the foot of the bed where her husband had once lain and which Mike had refused to leave for hours at a time. As she went on about these things, I saw that my mother was not, in fact, living alone.

No, we humans are not living alone on this earth. The earth teems with countless lives other than our own. If we listen, our hearts are always telling us this. We are well advised to slow down, be prepared to brake or swerve if nec-

REAL ESTATE

A morning in late May. Kneeling on the ground, I work a hand cultivator into the soil of the vegetable garden I keep in a remote mountain valley in northeastern California. The day warms; the shadows shorten toward noon. The soil turns up moist and dark beneath my hands.

All through the night while I slept, the planet revolved eastward, bearing this little western garden of mine back toward the sun, bearing the mountain night toward another day. The garden that comes to my hands today emerges out of a yesterday that has traveled the distance of two vast oceans and three continents in its daily journey to the present.

The plot I cultivate is a raised bed four feet wide and twelve feet long. It is one of sixteen such beds in the garden. Like the others, it was dug deep and screened for rock. Its soil is rich with compost and earthworms. My digging here this morning releases the scent of warming soil.

The garden is fenced against the deer who come out of the woods to feed in the open grassland where the garden is situated. Adjacent to the garden is a tool shed, a pumphouse, a well, and four compost bins. Down slope from the garden are a few apple trees and beyond these a house and garage finished in board and batten. The house opens onto a fenced yard landscaped with young trees and shrubs. A woodshed adjoins the garage. This household sits on twenty acres of grassland sloping from a pine woods down to the county road below.

All this is for sale. I had not intended to sell it, but circumstances now require that I do so. I know, of course, that it is perfectly ordinary to buy and sell property, yet something is terribly wrong here. I can scoop up some of this garden earth and, though it is just a fistful of dirt like all the other dirt it is nonetheless at this very instant, even as I cup it in my hands, spinning in orbit round the sun.

Nothing holds still here. We are all in a state of rapid transit, and if I weren't secured for the trip the whole twenty acres would be stripped from under me, and I would be in Asia by midnight. But this will not happen: we humans are held fast here for our dear lives. The planet too is held fast. The sun, the galaxies of suns, all the streaming, twisting entities of the universe are held fast, each secured somehow within the others. This quickened soil that I hold here in my hands owes its unlikely stability to sources as obscure as they are fantastic.

It is a dizzying proposition to think that I can sell such a thing. If I am to sell it, I must first own it. Apparently I do, for such ownership is recognized in a joint tenancy grant deed issued by Cal-Sierra Title Company for Plumas County parcel number 025-420-10. But what can it really mean to hold title to so active a thing? What exactly is it that I own? What is to be sold? What bought?

I ask these questions of myself because I know of no one else who will ask them of me. They are questions that need to be asked. *Real estate* has become our most common designation for the earth upon which we live, and its fair market value has become the common measure of its worth. We think of land as property, a commodity for exchange. We ascribe to its ownership certain rights to which we believe we are entitled.

For seven years now I have tended this garden. I broke the native sod and turned it under to rot. I screened the soil for rock and dug in manure. I composted and watered and seeded and harvested and returned all waste to the soil. I have done these things, yet I have been helpless to effect any outcome whatsoever except what the earth provides. And it provides not just a little, but all. The very body and mind with which I tend the earth are themselves of the earth. I am but earth tending earth. Were the earth not to roll this garden toward the sun today, were the clouds not to gather above the sea, the waters not flow, the soil not brim with its billions of micro-organisms, were all or any part of this to fail, I would fail as well, my body numbed to a fixed stillness, my slightest thought canceled.

This truth is so obvious that it is a wonder we can forget it so often and so easily. The fact of it defines who we are. To forget it is to forget ourselves, a society suffering from amnesia that, bewildered, seeks its own name.

It is right here in this garden that one can see how trivializing and irrelevant are the notions of property and property rights. This garden feeds me; it yields up life that I might have life. I am joined to this garden by an urgent

9

interdependence. The best any gardener can do is to harmonize his will to that of the earth. It is a teaching learned in humility and gratitude; it has no rights to press.

In marketing these twenty acres, I market myself as well. What I have to sell here is a relationship, one involving deep, critical responsibilities. The only property right I can actually transfer is the exact obligation of these responsibilities. This is the salient, sacred, soul-sustaining fact, and if I am to avoid one of life's most debilitating errors, I must hold this fact steadily in sight throughout the whole of this sales transaction. My body knows exactly how this stands; it taps directly into seven years bent to the task. Our bodies always know where we are even when we don't. Seasons rise and fall within us on blood tides of hunger. Sheer daily need roots our mouths to the subsoil. When we lose sight of this, the fundamental wonder of it still lies fallow in our very tissues to be called forth again as joy. This wonder, this springing joy, is our only health precisely because it is our only reality. Our sanity is measured by the presence in us of such wonder. Lose it and we go mad. We deal in real estate. We become incoherent with talk of "property" and "title" and "rights pertaining to thereof."

I can survive the sale of my mountain home if I negotiate the deal from the foothold I have here in this garden. I can come through this transaction with my mind intact if I never forget where I am and what I am doing. We humans have been entrusted to the earth, the earth entrusted to us. When we do not tune ourselves to this trust, the resultant discord is fatal. Our only true song perishes on the instant, even though we may seem to sing on endlessly.

I have a house to sell. In the meantime, I tend my garden.

LITURGIES OF VIOLENCE

*"Should they not as
well be taught some
ritual of atonement,
that their hearts
not harden
beyond regret?"*

THE KILLING SHED

I huddle by the tub of scalding water. Steam rises from its surface and a little warmth can be gotten from the gas jet underneath. Through the open door at the rear of the shed, I can see into the holding pen where forty or fifty turkeys stand jammed together in the rain. Their wings, heavy with rainwater, drag in the mud as they mill about and push themselves against the fence looking for a way out. In the shed, seven of them hang in a row suspended from the ceiling by cords cinched to their legs. Their feathers are smeared with mud and manure, and their necks are stretched toward the floor by lead weights hooked into their nostrils. Their bodies alternately relax and contract in sudden spasms. Blood drains from their bills into buckets beneath them.

I wear heavy yellow rain gear and rubber boots, splattered now with blood. In my hand, I hold a boning knife. It too is sticky with blood. Where some of the blood has soaked into a sleeve end beneath my rain jacket, I can feel a little of its residual warmth. The turkeys hang dead, the last of their convulsions over, their necks limp, their weighted heads gradually swaying to a stop, their eyes vacant above the bloody rims of the buckets.

At the sink, where the slaughtered turkeys will soon be gutted and dressed for sale, I wash the blood from my hands and from the boning knife. I lay the knife on a work bench alongside a cleaver and meat shears. I drag a ladder out from the wall to the center of the shed. The rain gear presses cold and stiff against my body as I climb toward the ceiling to take the turkeys down.

Fifty-five years have passed since those days in the killing shed. I was nine years old at the time, and I don't recall who in the family gave the shed that peculiarly accurate name. It was probably my father, a Danish immigrant, whose choice of English possessed a literalness that could sometimes expose the heart of a matter. The killing shed was part of a plan to get us out of the poverty we were left in by the Great Depression of the thirties. Father had gone into farming, which was what he had done in Denmark and the only thing he knew to do. He'd chosen to raise turkeys because it was something he could get into with almost no money for a start.

By the time of the killing shed, the farm had done pretty well. The idea was that we could make more money if we retailed holiday birds directly from the farm. An old garage and attached shed were adapted for this purpose. The garage became the salesroom and the attached lean-to the killing shed. Like everything else we did on the farm, this plan took the entire family to make it work. My mother, my eleven-year-old brother, Rowland, and I were put to the task.

One of my jobs was to help out in the killing shed.

Father had anchored seven eye bolts in a row across the ceiling of the shed. From these hung lengths of cord. On the floor below each of these seven stations were a bucket and a lead weight with a stiff piece of bent wire attached to it so that the weight could be hooked into the nostril of the turkey. The idea was to keep the turkey's head from thrashing about so that the blood drained into the bucket.

It was raining the day Father taught me to kill the turkeys. The two of us went out to the turkey yards in our rain gear and herded a bunch of them up to the killing shed and shut them into the holding pen Father had built there. Father grabbed a turkey by the legs and carried it into the shed. I did the same but, only nine years old and not very big for my age, I had to more or less drag mine in. Father hung his turkey up and went back for another. I hauled my turkey up the ladder we had put there for my use, but I couldn't get the cord wrapped around the turkey's legs because it kept flopping its wings, and I hadn't the strength to hold it in place long enough to get it tied. When Father saw this he said, "Okay, I'll put them up. You take them down afterwards." I liked that because it made our jobs equal. Father must have known how important I felt doing something as grown up and serious as killing the turkeys.

When all seven of the turkeys were hung, Father took the boning knife from the work bench. He grasped the head of one of the turkeys and stretched its neck down hard. He forced its bill open with his thumb and finger. Father told me to watch carefully, that the way to kill the turkey was to punch the point of the knife up through the roof of its mouth into its brain and then to slice the veins in its throat to start the blood flowing. Suddenly I saw the magnitude of what was going to happen. "Does it hurt?" I asked. "It's all over in a minute," he answered. I watched Father slide the knife into the turkey's mouth. I saw his wrist cock upward. The turkey exploded, its wings contracting violently. Its head jerked about in Father's hand, blood gushing from its throat. Father hooked the weight into its nostrils. The turkey's bill opened and closed. Its neck repeatedly contracted upward, causing the weight to sway about. Blood splashed into the bucket below. "Now you try it," Father said.

It was hard for me to force the turkey's bill open. "You have to push harder," Father said. I knew this but, as illogical as it might seem, I didn't want to squeeze down harder because I didn't want to hurt the bird. My hand shook and the knife was unsteady. I held my breath. I stabbed and sliced up into the throat. The turkey recoiled upward, its head slipping from my grasp, its whole body arching upward, blood spraying against the ceiling and on the walls and raining down on Father and me, our hair and faces splattered with it. Father got the turkey back under control and held it down until I could get hold of it again. "You have to hold tight," he said. "Is it dead?" I asked him. "Yes, it's dead, Linley," he replied.

When I had killed a second turkey, Father said, "I think you've got it now. Finish the rest and when they stop bleeding, take them down and put them on the work bench. I'll be back to show you what to do next." With that, he went out the shed door into the rain. The four remaining turkeys hung from the ceiling, waiting to be killed.

That first season in the killing shed was not the first killing I had done on the farm. It only marked an advance in something I had already become well acquainted with. One source of a great deal of killing on our farm was the process of culling injured and diseased birds from the flock. It was a process that began the day the chicks hatched and that lasted the whole of their short lives. Many of these culls were the result of cannibalism, a behavior unknown among wild turkeys but common in the crowded flocks of domestic poultry. I would find one of these victims standing helpless and near death while the others ate a hole into its side. If a culled bird could be saved, it was put in the sick pen. If it was beyond saving, it was put to death. I could not have been much older than six or seven when Father taught me how to do this.

We killed these culls by breaking their necks, grabbing them by the legs and base of the head and stretching until the neck snapped. The instant the neck broke, the bird would contract so violently that it was hard for even a grown man to hold on to. As a boy, I had to let go, and the turkey would thrash about in the dust and manure, and sometimes pitch itself against objects or even into the air.

We had lots of dead bodies to get rid of. To dispose of them, Father dug deep pits in the ground, and when one filled up, he dug another. It was a great labor to dig a pit; it took several days to complete. Because Father kept a second job during the day, he sometimes dug an entire pit in the dark after supper. When it was done, he would roof it over with wood beams and boards and drag a layer of dirt over it. In the center of this roof, he anchored a garbage pail with the bottom cut out and added a lid for opening and closing the pit. Wanting the pit to last as long as possible, he didn't lime the carcasses of the birds, but instead let the flies get to them so that the whole pit became a writhing mass of maggots consuming most of the bulk that was dropped to them. The smell of the pit was such that you couldn't even approach it without gagging. When I had a dead turkey to drop in, I would hold my breath and try to get the turkey into the pit and the lid clamped back before I had to run for air.

It takes a lot of strength to break a large turkey's neck. Since I started very young, Father put me to culling out birds from the younger flocks. The killing I was required to do was matched to my increasing capacity to do so: I graduated to older and larger birds as I myself got older and larger. It was a task that followed me throughout childhood until I finished high school and left the farm.

I never got used to it. There was a sympathy in me I could never still. I heard its voice every time I killed. My Father and even Rowland seemed to kill without noticing they were doing so. I'd see them snap the neck of a turkey and toss it to the ground without the slightest interruption in some conversation they were having. It was as if the action of their hands was disconnected from the rest of them. Seeing them do this, I felt isolated within my own troubled feelings.

At the time, as a Future Farmers of America project, I raised rabbits. I gave it up because I could no longer bring myself to kill the rabbits for market. It was also at this time that I fell desperately and distantly in love with the nine-year-old daughter of the Ranneys, who kept dairy cows on an adjacent farm. I loved her because the day she showed me the veal calves where they stood cramped upright in their solitary stalls, starved and unable even to lie down in their weakness, her eyes got suddenly wet and she had to look away. I took up those tears like a wilted plant starved for water. I would wait in the yard near her house, hoping to see her. At length, she asked me to stay away.

Afterwards, when I wasn't needed for work, I increasingly spent the hours alone. I had a spot I went to in the shade of a tree row beyond the farm, where the turkeys were out of sight. There I spent my time in daydreams. I sometimes imagined I was mounted on a powerful horse, white or black or chestnut, riding in the wind on a beach where the waves broke.

But these daydreams were shattered by an incident that occurred in my tenth year, the summer after I was first put to work in the killing shed. A few turkeys always managed to get out of their pens, and one of my jobs was to put them back. To do this, I had to catch them first and, if the turkey was especially large, it was sometimes nearly impossible for me to chase it down and get hold of it. This was the case one hot August afternoon when I tried to catch a large hen that had gotten out. I repeatedly drove her into a fence corner but, just when I thought I had her, she would break away. I had a summer cold and was short of breath, and I couldn't run her down. My nose ran and my head ached. Once again I drove the hen into the corner. This time I literally threw myself on her, grabbing for her legs. But I got only one leg, and the hen struggled to strip herself free with the loose claw. I felt my hand tear but I wouldn't let go. I tried to pin her against the fence but she scratched her way up the wire. A wing stung me across the eye. But I got hold of the wing and, still gripping the one leg I had managed to control, I raised her above my head and slammed her against the ground with all my might.

I still had hold of her when she struck. I felt the impact. I felt something break. She gasped with the shock of it. For a second neither of us moved. Then I felt her stir beneath my hands, struggling to get to her feet. I let go of her. Feathers came loose in my hands. When she tried to rise, I saw that she was grotesquely deformed, with one side flattened where bone ends showed beneath the skin. She repeatedly toppled back into the dust.

She was horribly injured. I would have to kill her. It was suddenly urgent that I do so. I caught her by the feet and the base of her head and stretched her neck as hard as I could, but her size was beyond my strength and her neck wouldn't snap. I stood on her neck and pulled on her legs with both hands. Still her neck would not break. I twisted and pulled on her neck until the skin ruptured beneath my hands and peeled itself, inside out, up over her eyes like a hood, leaving the flesh and tendons of her neck exposed. Still she was not dead.

A sudden sense of Father nearby. Had he seen? Could I get his help? I spotted him working in a field some distance away. I called to him. He didn't hear me. I thought of calling again. I thought of trying once more to break the turkey's neck, but I couldn't bear to touch her again. I ran from her, leaving her stumbling about in the dirt, blinded by her own skin.

I ran to the tree row beyond the farm. I sat in the fallen leaves and pulled my knees up tight to my chest and rocked myself. I bit my lip to keep from crying out. But I was hardly there a minute before I knew I had to go back. I needed help. I went looking for Father, an urgency rising in me to tell him what I'd done.

The turkey was gone, only a few loose feathers left scattered on the dirt. Father, too, was no longer in the field where I'd last seen him. When I located him cleaning manure trays in the brooder house, he spoke first. "I found an injured bird," I heard him say, "down by the breeder pens. I've put it in a coop behind the feed barn. I want you to see that it's kept in feed and water." The confession I had come to make died in my throat. I wiped my eyes on the back of a sleeve and went to get a water and feed crock.

I tended the turkey until it died. It stood in the corner of the coop. I never saw it move. The exposed flesh of its head and neck gradually blackened and crusted over. It never ate or drank. At the end of a week, I found it stiff on the bedding of straw I had spread there. It looked to me as if it had lain down to die.

At the pit, I took a deep breath and held it while I lifted the lid and dropped the turkey in. But then I did something I had rarely, if ever, done before. I looked down into the pit to see if I could see where the bird had fallen. Before my eyes could adjust to the darkness, I had to take a breath, which sickened me horribly. But, in the instant before I clamped the lid down and ran for air, I saw her there.

What lay on the bottom of the pit taught me, once and forever, what killing was. I have carried the knowledge of it like an unaddressed message that could not be delivered until I knew to whom it was to be sent. I deliver it now.

On farms across this nation, little boys—and no doubt girls too—are taught to kill for their needs and for the needs of others who are utter strangers to these acts performed on their behalf. They are further taught to dispose of whatever is weak, vulnerable, useless to their purpose. Should they not as well be taught some ritual of atonement, that their hearts not harden beyond regret? I would teach them pity; bring them to the sorrow that ever abides in the taking of things. I would shape their mouths to words of gratitude, teach their hands restraint, the gentle acts of mercy. I would commit their minds into the care of their own natural sympathies. I would have them know peace.

LIMIT

Everyone was catching fish except my mother and me. There were nearly two dozen of us jammed onto a narrow strip of mud between the parking lot and the water's edge, and everybody was hauling in trout. My mother wasn't catching any because she refused to switch her bait from salmon eggs to worms, and I wasn't catching any because I had brought a fly-fishing rod and refused to fish with any bait at all.

Except for a few who fished from boats in the deeper water, every one of us was congregated on this single spot of shoreline, not twenty feet from where we had parked our cars. You could feel the heat from the engines of the new arrivals where they pulled in behind us, the dust they raised from the clay parking lot settling on us like a dry fog. And then a newcomer would haul a plastic lawn chair and a fishing rod out of the trunk of his car, and addressing no one in particular and requiring no answer, he'd ask, "Well, what're they hitting on today? The usual?" But he'd already be threading a worm on the hook and eyeing a patch of uncontested water for his cast. By the time he folded his lawn chair out and sat down, he'd have his first catch.

The northern California college where I taught was

shut down for the summer, and I had driven south to Orange County to visit my parents. The two of them had recently taken up fishing, and no sooner had I arrived than they had me packed into the back seat of their car headed out to Irvine Lake for some fishing.

Had I remembered to bring my fishing rod, they asked before I was even inside the door. Their urgency, it turned out, was driven by the fact that Thursday, the day of my arrival, was also the day Fish and Game stocked the lake: if you wanted to catch fish, that's when you needed to get out there. That was also why we had to fish from the parking lot. That's where Fish and Game dumped the fish.

Ten fish was the limit at Irvine. We hadn't been there much over an hour before Father was within a couple of trout of limiting out. But he couldn't enjoy his good fortune because Mother was still without a single catch. Her stubborn insistence on using salmon eggs aggravated him. He wasn't pleased with me either. I couldn't motivate myself to fish at all under such circumstances. I spent the hour standing around with an idle fly rod in my hand, refusing Father's offer of a bait rod he had brought just in case I needed it. It lay unused in the trunk of the car not more than twenty feet away. This left Father torn between the pleasures of demonstrating his own skills at getting fish and his distress that I wasn't getting any of my own. He wanted me to have a good time.

The truth is I felt superior to him and to all the others as well. As congenial as I tried to appear, I secretly scorned the whole bunch of them, sitting on their plastic chairs, hauling in a limit of bewildered hatchery fish that knew nothing whatsoever about surviving in a lake and had never eaten a meal that wasn't thrown to them. I, after all, was a fly fisherman. I wouldn't degrade my sport with such easy takings. Still, I cheered Father on whenever he hooked a fish. He saw through the falseness of the gesture. He knew I disapproved of what he was doing. The knowledge of it showed in his eyes.

Father kept his catch on a metal stringer secured by a short length of clothesline to a stake he'd pushed into the mud at the water's edge. From time to time, the stringer floated ashore and beached itself. Father would heave it back out into deeper water, trying to keep the trout cool in the heat of the afternoon. With nine fish on the stringer, he was down to one more catch.

Seeing that his very prosperity had run him headlong into a sort of poverty, he was saving this last catch so as to have something to look forward to for the rest of the day's outing. He fussed with Mother over using some of her limit, since she hadn't used any of it herself and wasn't likely to as long as she kept to salmon eggs. But she didn't want to share. Still he kept after her; still she refused.

"You have your limit and I have mine, to use in any way we wish," she explained to him quite logically. She sat on her beach chair, her fishing line hanging undisturbed where it entered the water. Father sat beside her, staring stiffly ahead, his arms folded across his chest. All around them the others were dragging fish ashore. "But, Lucy, you're not using your limit at all. You haven't caught a fish." "Well then, it's my limit not to use at all, as you put it. I don't tell you what to do with your limit, why should you tell me?"

When I offered Father *my* limit, he turned me down. "Well then, how about splitting it. Five each?" "I don't want to do that, Linley," was all he said. I thought about the bait rod in the trunk of the car. It was all set up with fresh hooks and weights. Father had bought new line for it in anticipation of my visit. I felt awful. "Look, I think I'll check out the shallows at the outlet. I might do some good down there with bass flies," I explained. And then, for no other reason than that I couldn't seem to break it off, I added, "There might be some bass in the shade of the cottonwoods down there." And yet again, "Or in among those weeds and snags."

At the outlet, the lake narrowed into a long shallow pool where cottonwoods shaded the water. The bottom was weedy, and patches of water lilies floated on the surface. Clumps of willow overhung the banks. It was, as I had said, a good place for bass. But I didn't at once set out to fish. Some inexplicable reluctance restrained me. The outlet was the only wooded portion of the shoreline. All the rest was exposed to full sun, with withered grass and a kind of gray, stickery chaparral growing right down to the mud at water's edge. From the cool beneath the cottonwoods, I watched the group at the parking lot where they shimmered in heat waves that ran along the shore. I tried to make out my mother and father, but from such a distance their heat-distorted images were lost among the others. I felt—and this is the part that's hardest to account for—the deepest sudden tenderness for the whole wavery little group of them. Their cars, all lined up in the dust of the parking lot, looked sad and pitiful to me. It seemed for the moment as if everyone I had ever known was in transit somewhere, pausing briefly at the margins of some cooling place, trying just once more to extract an hour's respite from their cares.

There under the cottonwoods, a stillness rested on the water. From time to time a slight breeze wrinkled its surface. My skin and clothing smelled of the willows I had pushed through to get to the shore. Splashes of sun broke through the canopy overhead, illuminating pockets of water where waving stems of yellow and green bottom weeds stretched toward the surface. It reflected off the flutterings of butterfly wings and sparkled the waxy leaves of the water lilies. And it showed something else I would otherwise have missed. There, against the far bank, where a shaft of light penetrated the dark waters beneath the willows, a form moved among the weeds. I watched as it sank back into darkness. Then it reappeared. It was a largemouth bass and it looked simply huge. I had never seen the like of it anywhere in the county. Its presence confirmed what I had once been told: even though the lake had not been stocked for bass since before I was born, a few remnants of the original population still survived. I watched the shadow of the big fish as it moved in and out of the light. A gust of wind rippled the surface of the water. Dragonflies rested on the lily pads. Still I did not fish.

The sound of an engine shattered the quiet. A door slammed. I could see beyond the trees that a late-model pickup had stopped on a road I hadn't even known was there. Someone was coming down through the chaparral

toward me. I saw that it was a man, tall and broad shoul-
dered, and that he was walking not like one who is sizing up
a situation, but like one who knows exactly where he is
going and what he is going to do there. Chest waders were
slung over his shoulder. A creel and net hung at his waist.
He came in under the trees and pushed his way past the
willows to an opening on the bank not forty feet from
where I stood. Without a second's hesitation, he pulled on
the waders and stepped into the water.

I could see then that he carried a long, single-pieced
graphite fly rod with what looked like a bass popper tied to
the leader. He waded out into the water far enough to clear
some space for his cast. He threw the line back up over his
head, fed it out forward, threw it back again, out, back a
third time, and laid the popper right up the middle of the
pool. He waited while the rings spread out a bit, then
twitched the popper. Twitched it again. Again. But even
before he'd twitched it a second time, I saw the heavy shadow of the bass move out from the darkness of the willows.

The popper disappeared. The line straightened. The
man in the waders set the hook hard. With lots of pull
against the fish, he followed it down the length of the pool,
dragging water weeds behind him and churning up mud.
When the bass was netted, he walked back down the pool to
his point of his entry and was gone as quickly as he came. I
heard the pickup receding in the distance. I wasn't at all
sure he'd even known I was there.

It was the biggest bass I'd ever seen anyone catch, the
track of its conquest marked in mud and floating weeds. But
I couldn't discover in myself the excitement I ought to be

feeling. Instead, I felt disheartened. I turned to go, but just as I took my eyes from the water, something moved that shouldn't have. There, in the exact spot from which the bass had been raised, was the unmistakable shadow of a second fish. A great fish. A trophy like the first.

There was an instant of painful hesitation in which I almost walked away, but instead I tied a bass fly to my leader. I walked into the water in my pants and shoes and cast the fly as lightly as I could onto the leaves of the lilies where they floated against the bank. I waited until the shadow moved again into the light and then I twitched the fly into the water. The bass struck instantly, but no sooner had I hooked it than I knew I didn't want to kill the fish. But with the puritanically light leader I had always insisted on using, the bass exhausted itself and floated up dead before I could bring it to net. I held it under water, trying to revive it, knowing as I did so that it was no use, that I had killed the fish. Still, even in my regret, I marked the fact that the bass was not as big as the first.

Back at the parking lot everyone converged on me. None of them had ever seen a fish like it at the lake. They all agreed that it was "at least thirty inches if it's an inch." They hefted it to determine its weight, and estimates ranged from a modest seventeen pounds to an extravagant thirty-five. It seemed important to them to get the weight right, and various figures were put forth and disputed. It was as if I'd uncovered the treasure we'd all been looking for, and seeing it in hand, they wanted to know its exact worth. To a person, they were all glad for me, yet they envied me as well. After all, if it couldn't be one of them, at least someone got the prize. Even my father's eyes showed his hunger to have been the one. "A fish like that is limit enough for a lifetime of fishing," someone said.

But I no longer wanted to be the one with the trophy fish. I didn't want to believe that whatever it was that we'd been seeking all these years was measurable in inches and pounds. I didn't want to show up anyone else's catch, didn't want anyone's admiration or envy, didn't want to limit out ever again. For I had seen that getting your limit, no matter how tastefully it was executed, meant killing, and it meant killing for sport. It meant ten dead fish for the sake of a few hour's recreation. It meant snatching a load of miserable hatchery fish from the confinement of a concrete tank and tossing them into Irvine Lake on a Thursday morning so that my mother and father and I could converge on them in the afternoon and put to a quick end their first and only release into open water. It meant preferring at whatever cost dead fish to live ones. It meant witnessing two normally sane and reasonably compassionate people squabble over who would get to do the killing. It meant remembering, for half a lifetime now, how the stain of mud spread in deadly stillness over a pool where only moments before the clear waters quickened with the gliding shadows of ancient bass.

I gave the bass away to an old couple who dropped their protest when I convinced them that it would otherwise go to waste. It turned out that Mother and Father had resolved their dispute. Father had baited worms for Mother, a procedure she loathed doing for herself, and she had caught some fish and shared the rest of her limit. So now they had twenty trout on the stringer that they didn't want for themselves and would end up giving to neighbors. We loaded the fish into a tub in the trunk of the car, and all the while Mother lamented what a shame it was I couldn't take them home with me.

As we drove away, with me once again in the back seat, my clothes dripping lake water, I saw that the other Linley, the one who came to fish, still stood in the dust of the parking lot. I watched him until he was lost to sight. The last I saw of him he was looking down the shoreline to where the cottonwoods clustered around the outlet. For all his misgivings, sudden and unprecedented, he still coveted the larger of the two bass that had died there that afternoon. He wasn't at all sure now what to do with such feelings.

"It's a shame there isn't some way you could take these back to Monterey with you , Linley," Mother repeated.

"Yes," I replied, "it's a shame."

CANNONS

The story I begin with is a simple story.

In early July of this past summer, I had need of some hay to mulch the garden. Karen, my wife, and I drove out to the Roberti Ranch in Sierra Valley, California, to buy a half dozen bales. After the bales were loaded, we stopped at the main ranch house for a short visit. The three of us, Helen Roberti, Karen, and I, were sitting at the table in the big ranch-house kitchen when the conversation turned to what kinds of birds had been seen recently at the ranch. It was then I learned of the nest in the hat.

The hat, it turned out, belonged to Helen's grown son, Rick, who had earlier bought the hat to wear in the heat of summer. But the summer was already quite hot, and Rick was not wearing his new hat. A pair of house finches had appropriated it for a nesting site. The hat, in fact, was hanging exactly where he had hung it on a peg in his garage some months before.

Of course I had to see this for myself. Helen led Karen and me across the farmyard to the house where Rick and his wife, Carolyn, and their two children live. The garage door stood open because it couldn't be closed without obstructing the finches' access to their nest. The hat was a quality Bradford straw, tightly woven, bearing a smooth leather sweatband and shaped to western style. It was hung with its cavity toward the wall, but angled in such way that a small bird could get in and out. And sure enough, in the interior of the hat, on the surface that would have fitted to Rick's forehead had he been wearing it, a circle of grasses and twigs was being formed into a nest.

Outside the garage we ran into Rick, who had come from his chores to visit with us for a moment. Carolyn joined us from the house, holding their newborn daughter. We spoke of this addition to their family and of the garage finches and of other things that people speak of for the sake of knowing one another.

But as we stood on the graveled drive in front of the garage talking, I saw Rick in the light of this new disclosure, and it lent for me some strangeness to his presence. He was visually the same Rick as before, standing stout and muscled, his feet planted easily yet surely, a body that hoists bales onto flatbed trucks and works cattle in and out of a chute. Still, I felt a sense of starting all over again, back at the beginning, some inclination to say, "So you're Rick Roberti. I'm Lin Jensen. I'm glad to meet you."

A second story, one that followed my visit to the Roberti Ranch, brings complexity, even confusion, to an otherwise simple sequence of events. Although in retrospect I can see that some such incident was implied in my reactions to the first story, the juxtaposition of the two raised old questions that neither my intellect nor my heart knows exactly how to answer.

Recently we acquired new neighbors. They moved a

travel trailer onto their property, which is adjacent to our own, so that fewer than twenty acres separate the trailer from the garden for which I purchased the hay. I know little of these neighbors as yet, except that the husband and wife are fairly young. They have three children with whom they spend a great deal of time, for I can often hear their laughter and their calls to one another when they are out exploring their new property. It is to my discredit that I have not yet walked over to welcome them.

The week following my visit to the Roberti Ranch, I was busy one morning breaking open the bales of hay and spreading them in the garden. I had just put the wire cutters to a fresh bale when I saw the young husband come out of the trailer wearing camouflage pants, shirt, and cap of the sort that hunters wear. He carried a rifle that bore a scope, and I judged it to be of a caliber designed for larger game like deer or elk. He walked about in the clearing where the trailer was parked, holding the gun loosely in both hands, and from time to time he jerked the weapon up to his shoulder, squinting a practice aim.

I saw him then walk to where a brushy slope rose steeply from his property. Aiming into the slope, he snapped the rifle to his shoulder, lowered it, snapped it up again, lowered it. Then he brought it ever so slowly up to his shoulder, aimed, and fired. I heard the explosion in the chamber and the brief whine of the bullet before it thudded into the hillside. I heard this four more times as I saw him pan his rifle along the slope as though he were following the flight of a panicked animal.

I understood then that my young neighbor was

rehearsing for his sport and that his sport was killing. Those five squeezes of the trigger were his stated preference for death over life.

These circumstances could make for some really bad writing. The elements are those of propaganda, with contrasts too starkly opposed to seem credible. There I am mulching my garden with hay bought from a man who protects finches at the sacrifice of his hat while my neighbor shoots up the hillside with dreams of killing. Something radically divides here that ought to be kept whole.

Later in the summer, driving through Bridgeport, California, I stopped to check out the Mono County Courthouse, an antique structure set in a large expanse of lawn with great shading trees. Aside from the courthouse itself, the only other commemorative object at the site is an antique cannon of the sort used at the time of the Civil War. A plaque informed me that the cannon had been manufactured at the Standard Co. in nearby Bodie in 1931 and donated for placement at the county courthouse in that same year. "The cannon has never been fired," the plaque states.

At sixty-two years of age, I've done a fair amount of domestic traveling, so this virgin antique brought to mind a surprising number of small-town American city halls, courthouses, and parks on whose lawns I have seen just such cannons. What national love of weaponry has brought us to adorn our places of public gathering with historical instruments of death? The cannon displayed at Bridgeport features some actual cannon balls stacked and welded together so that they can't be carried off. They're quite large and made of solid iron. Seeing them there gives you some idea of the terror soldiers of the Civil War might have felt knowing such projectiles were hurtling toward their lines.

Everyone who has come to the Mono County Courthouse since 1931 to record a deed or vote or take out a marriage license, to pay taxes or record a birth, has passed by this cannon. Whatever their present purpose or frame of mind, they would have seen it there, its muzzle plugged tight with a cork of hardwood, the cannon balls welded into a useless clump. If an average of only ten people a day conducted business at the Mono County Courthouse since the cannon was first put there, that would be 229,950 of us with a cannon on our minds.

When I got back from my trip, I called the Robertis. Carolyn answered, and I asked her how the finches had done. "The babies grew so fast," she told me. "They were so tiny at first. But before we knew it, they were grown and had flown away. They kept the parents busy feeding them, I can tell you. Rick had to take the screen off the garage window so we could close the door. Maybe they'll come back next year." After a second's pause, she added, "Do you think they will?"

I answered, "I hope so."

MENDING

"And from that
very darkness
there rises in me
an unutterable
tenderness."

BAD DOG

THE JOURNEY THROUGH
SHAME TO COMPASSION

Within all light is darkness:
But explained it cannot be by darkness
that, one-sided, is alone.
In darkness there is light:
But, here again, by light one-sided
it is not explained.
Light goes with darkness:
As the sequence does of steps in walking.

—Sekito Kisen, *SANDOKAI*

1.

Shame is born of betrayal. It matters little whether one is victim or perpetrator, for shame adheres in the event itself, and all who participate are tainted by its presence.

I am eight years old, my brother, Rowland, ten. We follow our father up the steep wooden stairs to the second-story bedroom. He does not speak. Our steps echo in the hollow of the stairway enclosure. Father holds the lath stick by its end. It's stiff and splintery and it hangs from Father's hand almost to the floor. I am sick with dread. I swallow the words that would beg Father, once more, not to do this.

In the upstairs bedroom, Father shuts the door behind us. A ceiling light hangs from a cord. It lights the surface of the bed, leaving the corners of the room in shadows. Father stands by the bed. He looks at us. Rowland and I stand backed up against the closed door. We do not move. Outside in the hall, Laddie, our farm dog, scratches at the door. Father looks sad and serious like he wishes we didn't have to do this. He points toward us with the lath stick, and I hear him ask, "Which of you goes first?"

Rowland goes to the bed. He wants to get it over with. It's worse to go last, but I can never make myself go first. Rowland unbuttons his jeans and pulls them down to his knees. He does this without being told. He knows he has to pull his jeans and underwear down and lie face down on the bed. He pulls his underwear down at the very last because he doesn't like to show himself. He waits for the first blow. I look away. My body shivers and I feel cold. I hear Laddie snuffling at the door, and then I hear the crack of the stick. Rowland doesn't cry. He holds his breath. He has told me that this is the way to do it.

I hear the lath again and then again. Still Rowland doesn't cry. Laddie whines at the door. I don't know why Father is whipping us. Rowland teased me and punched me behind the barn, and I called him bad names. Did Mother hear us? I had some bad thoughts. Did Mother know them? Mother was angry and then she was sick and lay on her bed and put a wet cloth over her eyes and told us that we would be whipped when Father got home. I got scared and tried to talk to her and make it okay again, but the cloth was over her eyes and she wouldn't talk to me.

Rowland's turn is over and he gets off the bed. I pull my shirt up and tuck the end of it under my chin to keep it from falling. I pull my pants and underwear down. My penis feels rubbery where I try to hide it under my hands, and Rowland watches me. I hold my breath. The first blow comes. It hurts more than I can stand. My hands stretch back to cover my bottom and I hear myself whimpering, "Please, Father, please."

"If you do that, you'll only make it worse," Father warns.

When it's over, Father goes out. Rowland is in the dark near the wall. I'm under the ceiling light. Rowland can see me wiping at my runny nose with my shirt, but he looks away. We have something wrong with us. We both have it. We do not like to look at one another. It makes us too sorry. In a moment or two, Rowland goes out. The door shuts behind him and I hear him go down the stairs.

After a while I go out. Laddie is waiting. He's glad to see me and wags his tail and pushes himself against me. "Go away, Laddie," I say. Later, in the dark when I can't sleep, I slip from my bed and open the door onto the hall where Laddie waits. Clutching him to me, I tell him how sorry I am.

2.

Shame is felt as a failure of love. Its peculiar anguish lies in this perception.

I am eleven years old. Laddie has done something bad and Father has seen him do it and I don't know what is going to happen. Rowland says that Laddie killed a turkey. When the neighbor's dog killed a turkey, Father shot it. I saw him do it. The neighbor's dog whined and went round and round in circles until it fell down. Blood came out of its nose and pretty soon it died.

In the barn, Father has a rope around Laddie's neck. When Laddie tries to pull away, Father jerks the rope. It chokes Laddie and makes him cough. Laddie's fur is tangled and dirty like he's been dragged on the ground. A turkey lies dead on the floor. It's torn and bloody and its feathers are wet. "Oh Laddie," I cry out, "what have you done?" I squat and put out my hand. Laddie wags his tail and comes toward me.

Father jerks him away with the rope. "Don't be good to him, Linley," Father says. "Now that he's tasted blood, it's not likely he'll quit."

"He doesn't know, Father." I try not to cry, but I can feel my face screw up and voice goes high. "Please, Father, please."

Father hands me the rope tied to Laddie's neck. "If he kills again, he goes. Do now exactly as I say."

Laddie is tied by the rope to a post in the barn. I have gathered the bailing wire and wire cutters and roofing tar that Father told me to get. I'm supposed to tie the turkey around Laddie's neck. I'm supposed to paint the turkey with tar so that Laddie can't chew it off. It has to stay there until it rots. Father says we have to do this because, if I want to keep Laddie, we have only one chance. I'm not supposed to be good to Laddie. He has to learn not to kill.

The dead turkey is covered with flies. Tiny yellow eggs are already stuck to the places where the blood has dried. I take a stick and dab tar on the turkey until its feathers are all plastered down and the torn places are filled and its eyes are stuck shut. I punch the baling wire through its body and wrap one end around each of its legs so that I can tie them around Laddie's neck.

I take the rope off Laddie. He's glad to have the rope off and wags his tail and tries to lick my face. "Bad dog," I tell him, "bad dog." I tie the turkey around his neck. The turkey weighs his head down and the tar sticks to his fur. "Bad dog," I repeat.

After three days, mother won't let Laddie near the house anymore. We are told to keep the yard gates shut. "It's intolerable," she tells Father. "I can smell him even here in the house."

I watch Father. He doesn't look up and he doesn't say anything.

"It's not just the smell, you know," she says. "I can't bear the thought of it."

"That doesn't help any," is all Father says.

At the end of a week, Laddie quits coming for the food I carry out to him. I find him where he has crawled back into a space under the floor of the storage shed. I call to him but he won't come. I push the food under to him. I bring a basin of water and push it under too. I do this for two more weeks. Sometimes a little of the food is gone and some water but most of the time nothing has been touched.

Once during this time I see from a distance that Laddie

has come out from under the shed. The turkey sags from his neck and drags on the ground when he walks. Even from far away I can see that the turkey is slimy and bloated. "Laddie," I call. I run to him but, before I can get to him, he crawls back under the storage shed. I see him there in the dark. "Laddie, I'm sorry." I try to crawl under the shed to him but it's too tight and I can't reach him. "Laddie," I say again.

And then one day he's out. I find him in the barnyard, the baling wire still wound around his neck where the turkey has rotted off. I remove the wire, but he doesn't wag his tail or try to lick me. He doesn't do anything at all. I take him to the washroom and fill the washtub with warm water. I lift him into the tub and wash him with soap. I scrub him and rinse him and draw more water and wash him again. I dry him with a towel and brush him, and I keep telling him that it's okay now, that it's all over. I let him out on the lawn by the house where the sun shines through the elm tree, and then I go back to clean up the washroom.

When I come for him, he is gone. I find him under the storage shed.

3.

Shame bears within it the source of its own healing, for shame grieves the loss of love. Shame is this very grief whose tears flow from the eyes of compassion.

I am sixty years old. Father is ninety-three, and he is in the hospital with pneumonia. It is not at all certain that he will survive this illness. Rowland and I take turns watching him through the night. Now it is nearly two in the morning and Rowland has gone to rest. Father is fitful. He suffers from diarrhea, and it wakens him frequently in such a state of urgency that I do not dare doze off myself. Father is embarrassed to use a bedpan, and he is too weak to reach the toilet by himself. He needs me to get him there.

I watch him on the hospital bed where he labors in his sleep to breathe, his thin chest struggling with effort. Father is much softened with age and with grandchildren and great-grandchildren whose innocent love has reached him beyond his fears. They have coaxed him out of his darkness.

A quarter past three. Father calls. "Linley, I need to go." He tries to sit up and get his feet to the floor even before I can reach him. I help him up. He has so little strength, yet he uses every bit he has to get himself to the bathroom. I support him as we walk around the foot of the bed and through the bathroom door before I realize we are too late. His hospital gown is pulled open in the back and feces runs down his legs and onto the linoleum where he tracks it with his bare feet.

He looks at me with the most urgent appeal. He is humiliated by what he has done, and his eyes ask of me that it might never have happened. I back him up to the toilet and sit him down. A fluorescent ceiling light glares down on us. In the hallway beyond these walls, I can hear the voices of the night nurses on their rounds. I shut the bathroom door, and when the latch clicks shut on the two of us, the sound of it sends a shiver through me. Once again I wait for the crack of the lath stick. This old man, sitting soiled in his own filth, disgusts me. I cannot move myself to help him.

Then the sight of him blurs beyond sudden tears. Laddie whines somewhere in the dark. And from that very darkness there rises in me an unutterable tenderness.

"It's okay, Father," I tell him. "It's okay." I find clean towels and a washcloth and soap. I run water in the basin until it is warm. I take off his soiled hospital gown and mop the floor under his feet with it and discard it in a plastic bag I find beneath the sink. I wash Father with soap and warm water. I wash him carefully, removing all the feces from around his anus and in the hair on his testicles and down the insides of his legs and between his toes. I wash him as though I were washing my very own flesh, until all the rotten things are washed away.

In the morning, Father breathes easier. He survives another year until his death on the eighth of December, 1993.

4.

I have written of these things out of gratitude so that others might know, as I have come to know, that pain summons its own healer. You do not have to seek outside yourself for deliverance. If shame is all you have, embrace what you have, honor it, and care for it with all your attention and kindness. In your own grief you will find the power to convert shame to compassion.

LEARNING
TO SWIM

*Whenever one speaks kindly to
another his face brightens and
his heart is warmed; tenderness
can have a revolutionary impact
upon the mind of man.*

—Dogen Zenji, *SHOBOGENZO*

He was a chubby little boy with a puffy face that made his eyes look unusually small. He had a short thick neck and hair sheared close to the scalp. His fat little hands clutched the concrete wall of the river pool.

"Just let go, for Christ's sake!" his father ordered.

His father stood at the pool's edge directly above the boy, so that when the boy looked up, he saw his father from an angle virtually under the parent's feet. The father too was stout and thick-necked. He wore shorts and a T-shirt and a baseball cap. He stood in clogs of some sort with his thick legs spread apart and his feet turned outward. His arms were crossed over his chest.

"Just let go!" his father bellowed again. "God, the water's barely over your head!"

The boy's mother stood in the water where a set of steps descended from the wall into the pool.

"You can let loose now," she instructed the boy in a tone of contained sternness. "Let loose and swim to me."

Twenty feet separated the mother from the boy where he still clung to the wall. She inched toward him a foot or two.

"Look, I'm closer now. You've swum this far before."

"Why don't you just hold his hand while he does it?" the father said in disgust. "He can hang there all day for all I care," he added. He turned his back and walked away.

"Just let go!" the mother insisted, an anxious fear rising into her voice.

In all this, the boy had not spoken a word. His knuckles were white where they gripped the wall, and he had begun to shiver so hard from cold or fear that I thought he might shake loose into the water. I happened to be close at hand swimming when all of this took place. I pushed my way through the water to where the boy held on, which put me between him and his mother.

"It can be really scary to let go, can't it?" I said to him.

That's all I said, nothing more, yet I saw those words go right into his body, there where he clutched at the wall. Something in him yielded on the instant, as though I had done much more, as though I had lifted him to safety.

"I won't let you sink," I told him.

For the first time, he looked at me. Then he gauged the distance between himself and my outstretched hands, let go, and scrambled through the water toward me. His fat little hands closed on mine and held on fiercely. I floated him to where his mother waited on the steps. She met my eyes without disclosure of any sort.

Later, as I waded in the river shallows, the boy was suddenly there. I saw his mother and a girl who was apparently his sister nearby.

"You like walking in the water?" I asked.

He did not answer. But wherever I went he followed, and he came a little nearer by degrees until we were actually side by side. Without a word, he was telling me that he liked being near me, and when we came to a spot where the river moss made the footing slippery, he reached out to my hand for help.

I saw then how it was. I saw how the slightest tenderness, the merest sliver of acknowledgment, had won from him an affection and trust his parents daily forfeited in their sad ignorance. Neither of them understood that their child was on the verge of drowning.

From the distance his mother called to him to come away. Her voice reached us hard and sharp, provoked perhaps by his attachment to me, distrustful perhaps of my motives. The boy showed no sign of having heard her. She called again.

"Your mother's calling," I said to him. "You'd better go back."

I saw him shut down. His eyes, suddenly wary, looked at me out of his puffy face as if I had sent him into deep water. He turned away and walked disconsolately back toward his mother where she waited in sourness with her hands on her hips.

"You come when I call you," she scolded.

Perhaps she would not have scolded him so had she known that the boy was struggling to reach the surface and that he was giving all he had to the effort. But she did not know this, as most assuredly her husband had not known it earlier when he stood spread-legged at the pool's edge and ordered the boy to swim.

I watched them go, the mother, still scolding, heading back toward the pool with her daughter in tow, the boy trailing after them. My heart hurt for this little boy who must learn to swim in waters so dangerous he might sink from our sight at any moment.

HOME AND HOMELESSNESS

"I could no longer conceptualize who I was and, in that loss, the healing had begun."

Maintenance

*Here born, we clutch at things
and then compound delusion,
later on, by following ideas.*

—Sekito Kisen, SANDOKAI

These words are being written from a room in a house that has recently become for me a temporary residence. The walls and ceiling of the room are covered in rare and beautiful vertical-grained Douglas fir, all heartwood, rescued from a fire-burned ridge in the Santa Cruz Mountains of northern California. The windows and doors are framed of clear, kiln-dried redwood. The floor is laid with $7^1/_2$ x $3^1/_2$ x $1^1/_4$-inch Spanish-red paving bricks underlaid by an inch of mortar, small-mesh wire, 30-pound felt, and a tight subfloor. Each brick, 3,460 of them, was lifted by hand and grouted in place by my wife, Karen, and me. Every wall and ceiling board, every inch of trim, was milled and cut and nailed in place by the two of us. From the first spadeful of rocky earth torn loose to allow for its concrete footing, to its cabinets and bookshelves that now hold all the personal possessions either of us owns, this house was built by we who were to live in it and who would come in time to know it as "home."

But now, only six years since the Plumas County building inspector signified that our work was finished and that Karen and I could move in, a sign has been posted at the entrance to our drive declaring to all who travel Plumas County Road A-23 that the house we built is for sale. I can see the sign from our kitchen window. It is about four feet by four feet, tacked to a post and crossarm and, though it faces away from me toward the road, I know its message by heart:

LYNN	20 ACRES
WELCH	CUSTOM
REALTY	SOLAR HOME

LYNN WELCH REALTY
HWY 70 – PORTOLA CA
(916) 832-4455

When Karen and I retired, she from a hospital pharmacy and I from teaching and carpentry, we had thought to live out the remainder of our lives on these twenty acres, in this house, within walls grown as familiar to us as our own aging images in the mirror. But now, whenever I return from some outing with a load of groceries or gas for the snowblower or whatever, Welch Realty is there to remind me that I am once more a person in transition.

The place has already been shown a few times. When prospective buyers come to look at our home, we point out everything good about it, including the yard that Karen landscaped so beautifully and the vegetable plot with its sixteen raised beds and the compost bins and garden shed and even the woodshed where cords of firewood are so conveniently stacked. We fairly glow with custodial enthusiasm, so naturally we are sometimes asked why we are leaving. The question always strikes dead center (as its consideration does now), and I find myself avoiding the eyes of the questioner, offering up the obvious and plausible response: a recent injury to my spine prevents me from continuing the heavy work of maintaining the place.

What I don't tell the questioner and what the meeting of our eyes might give away is that I regret not doing the things that need doing, things Karen and I have always done together. I do not tell my questioner of how the demands of this place measure with distressing accuracy the exact extent of my daily inadequacies. I do not tell of the loss that this evokes in me. I tell of it now because I wish to show how loss itself cancels the source of its own distress.

That loss can heal wounds of its own infliction so that it is the wounding itself that heals was first revealed to me when I was much in need of healing. This knowledge came to me in late November of this past winter. I was lying in bed in the room adjacent to where I now sit. With the exception of the most necessary movement, I had lain exactly there since, doubled over in pain, I had limped into the house nine weeks before. My legs, basically useless to me, were propped up on pillows in a futile effort to ease the pain that was perpetually with me. Throughout those days, I could hear Karen moving about in the other rooms, hauling in armloads of firewood, shoveling snow away from the outside doors and digging her way to the woodshed so that she might haul in wood again, and then mopping her own muddy tracks off the floor. I could hear her cooking and washing up and carrying kitchen waste to the compost bin and doing these things again and again and again. Beyond all this, I had no option but to watch her care for my needs as well, bringing me water and food and tablets of codeine, endlessly bringing me these things day after day, night after night, week after week. And still in the early morning, when she herself was hopelessly exhausted, she would try, just this once more, to rub the pain away.

I could do nothing to ease the burden on her. I could do nothing at all. And I knew (for I had been explicitly told so) that when the surgery I was awaiting had restored me to my feet, much that I had always done I would never do again: "No weights over twenty-five pounds, no repetitive movement of an extended duration, no twisting, compacting, or sudden bending of the spine." I would never again do any sustained carpentry or turn clover under in the garden or drag up a few bales of hay for mulching or split wood. I would never backpack or turn a somersault or jump to the ground from even the most modest height or run the length of half a block. I lay in bed, looking up at the ceiling Karen and I had nailed in place, and I realized that if I were not that person who nails ceilings, I had no idea who I was.

One nails a wood tongue-and-groove ceiling in place while standing on planks laid across sawhorses. A partner helps secure the board in place. The nailer bends backward, pushing the groove hard onto the tongue with one hand while driving the nail with the other. That was now impossible. I had to let it go. In the instant of that yielding, a sweet, sad calm swept through me, and I was shown something I had not noticed before.

I saw that I had tried to build my life as I had built this house, with some fixed and lasting sense of myself nailed securely in place. I saw that no life so constructed could be held secure against the exigencies of time and circumstance, that I must inevitably exhaust myself in futile maintenance of such a structure. A lifetime of certainties fell about me in disrepair. I could no longer conceptualize who I was and, in that loss, the healing had begun.

We invent ourselves that we might know who we are and what we are to be. But the consistency we seek in these inventions cannot be maintained against the fabulous inconsistency of actual life. Sensing this, we clutch at our cherished constants ever the more urgently. I am weary of maintenance now. The builder of the house of ego can never rest, for he is ever at work to wall out alternatives and limit space. His structure makes its appeal to our longing for the familiar and the safe. In the end, he delivers only diminishment.

Knowing we must move on, Karen and I recently drove over the mountains to see if Chico, California, might be a place for us to live. The town has a state university, and Karen thinks she would like to go back to school for a while. Of course, there's much adventure in an excursion like this, yet at times we both felt a little forlorn. The motel room was unfamiliar, its papered walls not those of our own making. The toilet was sealed sanitary with a strip of paper assuring us of this precaution that some stranger had taken on our behalf. The towels smelled of some alien detergent or softener we were unaccustomed to. And when we sought out the weather channel on a TV so awkwardly hung as to be viewable only while lying on the bed, the meteorologist bore a face we did not recognize.

But we persisted in our intent and were able to join a small group of local residents on a wildflower outing to nearby Table Mountain. On the mountain we walked with the others on a windswept plateau where tiny flowers of yellow and blue hugged the rocky earth. Karen and the other women talked among themselves, and when they turned down along a little stream toward a falls, I was drawn uphill to see what species of sparrow it was that moved so low among the grasses. The birds turned out to be lark sparrows. Trailing after them, I found myself on a prominence that lay an unobstructed horizon about me on all sides. I turned slowly, 360 degrees. In all that space there was nothing, not even a trace of the very steps that had brought me there, to suggest where one might go next. I understood then that I could, at that moment, walk in any of all possible directions.

Later that evening Karen and I sat opposite one other in a strange restaurant trying to select something to eat from an uncertain menu of no acquaintance. I saw, even in the dim lighting of the room, the silent tears spread down from Karen's eyes.

"What is it?" I asked.

"I don't even know who I am," she answered.

I said, "I know."

MARGIE'S ROOM

When the door is closed, I don't go in without knocking. She's taking classes at the local college, and she might be studying and not want to be disturbed. She might be looking out the window, watching a neighbor or a passing car or sparrows flying in and out of the pistachio tree. She might simply want to be alone. It's understood between us that it is her room to do with as she pleases. She has sole control over the space, an authority to which I give my full respect.

When I first met Karen Laslo, I knew nothing at all about Margie. So I did not know that Margie had never had a room like the one Karen now has. I didn't have a room myself at the time. Instead, I lived in a small travel trailer on a ridge above California's Big Sur coastline. On the afternoon Karen first came to the ridge, we walked up Turner Creek into the Ventana Wilderness. We were just getting to know one another, and it was becoming clear to both of us that our feelings were more than merely friendly. We were made a little self-conscious by this fact, but as the afternoon wore on, we felt more and more easy in each other's presence. We walked holding hands, and we spoke intimately of things in the way old friends sometimes do.

But toward evening when we stopped back at the trailer for a cup of coffee, Karen seemed suddenly apprehensive about entering the trailer at all. She sat stiffly at the little fold-down table while I heated water. I asked if she were all right, and she explained that she felt "ambivalent" about me living in a trailer. The disclosure was so designedly obscure that I did not press for further explanation.

In time Karen Laslo and I knew we loved each other, and we became lovers. But Karen never stayed the night at the trailer. If we spent the night together, it was at her place in the nearby seaside town of Pacific Grove. Karen's apartment was above a garage, barely four hundred square feet. From the front windows I could see a thin sliver of Monterey Bay between the intervening houses. As a second story, it caught plenty of sunlight. I liked it there.

Karen liked it too, but from the start she showed signs of confinement. And this was only aggravated when we began to plan for our wedding and I moved in. If you divide a twenty-by-twenty-foot area into a kitchen, dining nook, living room, bedroom, closet, and bathroom, you have little space left for movement and none whatever for privacy. All I wanted at the time was to be with Karen, so I suffered no distress from the crowding. But Karen did. It was hard not to get in her way. At times she would grab for a jacket and head out the door, whatever the weather or hour. I could literally see her pulled back and forth between wanting me there and an equal need to have me out of there so that she could breathe some air of her own.

Nevertheless we decided to keep the apartment. Housing in the area was expensive and the apartment was a third the cost of any other rental we priced. We planned to build our own house in a few years and needed to save whatever we could. Karen saw the sense of this, but still she searched the classifieds in hopes of finding another rental we could afford. Sometimes, at her urging, I went with her to look at places that were clearly beyond our present means. Karen knew this, yet she examined the kitchen for cupboard space, noted what size table the dining area would accommodate, and measured the living room for furniture we didn't own. She inventoried each bedroom. This one would be ours, this for guests, this for a study. Heading back to our apartment after such outings, she was often subdued. After a little bit, she might say, "It was a pretty nice house, don't you think?"

Karen often spoke of having friends in for supper at the apartment, but the invitation was seldom given. I learned something of the source of this contradiction one day when she said to me, "I wish we had a place where we could have people in." Before I was able to ask her why we couldn't, she added, "I'm thirty-seven years old and I still live like this." I looked at the apartment. It was as attractive as we could make it, and yet I saw then that Karen was ashamed to be living there. At the time I did not know the deeper roots of her feelings.

It was in this same apartment that I discovered Margie. Karen and I were in the process of getting a marriage license, and we needed birth certificates. Karen sent for a copy. Now that the document was coming she seemed compelled to explain something before it arrived. She told me her actual first name wasn't Karen. And here I saw her falter, saw her swallow, saw how hard it was for her to look me in the eyes. Karen, she went on, was really her middle name. Her first name was Margie. She'd switched to Karen when she was eleven years old. She told me this simple thing with an air of seriousness that I could not account for.

When her birth certificate came, Karen was completely matter-of-fact, handing it to me as if it were of no consequence at all. The certificate recorded the birth of Margie Karen Laslo to her parents, Francis and Eloise Laslo, on February 20, 1947, in Nyack, New York. Who was this little Margie, I wondered, who had drawn her first breath thirty-seven years before in the maternity ward of Nyack General Hospital and whose record of birth I now held in my hands? What went wrong that she discarded her name and put herself out of sight?

In early June 1984, six weeks before Karen and I were wed, I was to see for myself where Margie was living when she disappeared. On a patch of bare alkaline ground in a trailer park southeast of Death Valley, California, Eloise and Frank Laslo still live in the same trailer they have occupied since Karen was a baby. Throughout the whole of her childhood and adolescence, this trailer, wherever it was parked at the moment, was Karen's only home. I was the first to see it. None of the men Karen had known had ever gone there. None had ever met her parents. Karen was terribly apprehensive about our visit. She tried to prepare me and thus told me things she had hoped she would not have to tell.

She told me of a father who pried into everything personal, who ordered his wife and daughters and son to do his bidding, who bullied and struck out in rage when they failed to do so, and who sunk into depressions from which he could not extricate himself. She told me she had never taken a friend home from school because she didn't want anyone to see how she lived. She told me of the nights she and her mother and sister and brother took refuge in a neighbor's spare bedroom or a motel room to wait out the times of humiliation and danger. She told me of the summer train journeys to the home of her maternal grandparents, William and Mary Kirby, her mother shipping the children to safety where they could be kids for awhile and where Karen could pretend she'd never have to come back to the trailer again. When Karen and I passed over the Tehachapi Grade into the desert that June, Karen had not seen her parents for ten years. We were traveling into the past.

We found the trailer in row E, space number 8, of the Yolo County Park at Tecopa Hot Springs, a few miles from the crossroads settlement of Tecopa, California. What I first saw made me swallow hard. The trailer had slumped down on its supports as though gravity itself threatened to pull it under, the tires having long ago rotted beyond use. Its sides were chalky white, like the alkali dust that spotted the ground of the trailer park. I had to squint to look at it in the afternoon light. The roof was covered with discarded automobile tires painted silver to reflect the sun. With few windows, it looked more like a big metal box than a place where someone lived. In mid-June, the trailer stood alone in the shimmering heat, the others having left the park to escape the blistering temperatures.

Inside the trailer, all one could do was sit down. There

simply wasn't room enough for people to move around. Everyone blocked everyone else's way. If one person needed to move, others had to move as well. Karen's mother, Eloise, sat the two of us at a small table shoved against a wall just inside the door. Once we were in place, she unloaded some boxes of cereal from the top of a stool and pulled the stool up to the table and sat down herself. Eloise Laslo had grown heavy over the years and she moved as if in pain. I offered her my chair, but she told me it was easier for her to get up from a stool.

Frank Laslo sat where he had been sitting for years, in a frayed upholstered chair with the fabric worn through on the armrests. From there he could watch television. Half a lifetime before, when Karen was still a child, Frank Laslo, driving his milk truck in the rain in the San Fernando Valley, saw through the splatters on his windshield the figure of a woman entering the street. He swerved to miss her, and the truck, with no side doors and no seat belt, rolled over. After the surgery and the therapy, and after he was restored to his feet, Frank Laslo made the fatal decision to be an invalid. He collected his monthly disability check and never worked for wages again. By the time I met him, his life was an endless round of TV game shows.

He was exactly as I had pictured him, a big man, gruff in manner, with large hands and dark, heavy eyebrows. I could see that he was trying to be sociable for our visit. But I felt how much of a strain it was for him. There was a dark brooding about him that he could not hide. He sat in his chair and from time to time interjected some brief comment into the conversation, but he seldom took his eyes from the television screen. He spoke in quick short jabs like a boxer who had backed himself against the ropes and was trying to punch his way out. His comments were mostly complaints, which Karen pointedly ignored.

I felt a tension between them that had the capacity to explode. Karen's mother felt it too; the fear of it showed in her eyes. This was the daughter who had defied her father, who had so hated his bullying that she had refused to be intimidated by it. I sat at the table with the three of them, the afternoon heat gradually overwhelming the trailer's inadequate cooling system, and I tried to imagine what it must have been like to live here. The trailer had less than three hundred square feet of living space, and much of that was taken up with household items for which there was no storage available. How did Frank and Eloise Laslo and their son and two daughters survive all those years within its confines?

That night Karen and I camped at a nearby oasis. The next day we drove Frank and Eloise to Parumph, Nevada, for shopping and supper. Eloise sat in the back with Karen. Frank rode up front with me. We had just started up the grade to Parumph, when Frank told me to pull over. "Over there," he said, "by those cliffs. Where the tree is. I want to show you something." I parked the car in the shade of the big palo verde tree he had pointed to and we got out.

"We'll be back," he said to Karen and Eloise, as if it were understood that he and I would go alone. What he wanted to show me was a room someone had laboriously carved into the soft rock of the cliff face. The room was about eight feet square with a ceiling so low one had to stoop. Timbers had been fitted to the entry to accommodate a door. When we'd both squeezed inside, Frank said, "There's a guy lived right here for fifty years. He's in books. He made everything. Nothing here but rock when he started. Didn't ask for nothing. Lived here till he died. It's all in books. I forgot his name, but this place is famous." I could see that Frank wanted me to be impressed. He stood there, his head scraping the dusty ceiling, envying the work of a man of some forgotten name who had chosen for the better part of a lifetime to bury himself in a hole in the ground. "It's a hell of a house, isn't it?" he said. "Yes, Frank," I answered, "it's a hell of a house."

By the end of the day civilities had worn thin. Frank had had all he could handle. All of us had had all we could handle. We crowded into the trailer for a last cup of tea. Karen and I planned to leave the next day. Frank sat silent, watching the TV. Eloise was weary with her own apprehension. None of us had much left to say. I thought to myself that it was to this father and to this trailer that Margie had returned each day from school. It was here at the age of eleven that she had ceased to exist because she no longer wanted to be who she was. She told everybody that her name was Karen and not to call her Margie anymore.

Much has happened since our visit to Tecopa. Eloise left her husband after a violent incident, taking refuge in a county shelter and swearing that this time she had left for good. But, as so many times before, she was back again in a few months, eyeing her husband warily, not really knowing how to live any other way. Karen and I married and in a few years saved enough money to build ourselves a small one-bedroom house in a mountain valley in northeastern California. Before seven years had passed, circumstances required that we sell the place and move again. The gain from this sale enabled us to buy the house in which we now live. The day the realtor showed us the house, Karen, as she had done twelve years earlier, inventoried the bedrooms. This one would be ours; that one for guests. "That leaves two more. We can each have a room! Can I have this one for mine?"

One day not long ago, on her way out to meet a friend, Karen invited me to sit in her room. "It's nice the way it catches the morning sun," she said. "You can read your book there." I took her up on the offer. I closed the door as Karen sometimes does. I sat in her chair and pulled it up to the writing table where she studies for her classes. She was right, it was nice. The room is not very big but there are two large windows that open onto the front lawn and a plot where gardenias and daphne grow. Even with the door closed, I didn't feel confined. Besides a writing table and the castered swivel chair I sat on, the room is furnished with a graceful upholstered chair on elegant hardwood legs, a foot stool, and a wonderful old floor lamp that Karen plans to restore. On the wall hangs a small picture of a country snow scene that long ago hung on the wall in the home of Mary Kirby, Karen's maternal grandmother. Alongside the snow scene hangs a framed copy of a 1929 calendar given out by Grandpa Kirby to customers of the West End Garage in Walker Valley, New York, ninety miles up river from Nyack where Margie was born.

Among her things on the writing table is a color photograph of Karen as a child. It is no larger than a snapshot and it's held in a gilt-edged frame. With the exception of the faint green tint of her sweater, all the details have faded to a sort of pinkish-red hue. The girl in the photograph sits on a boulder in a stream. I can see a swift current of water bending around the boulder and rapids in the background. The little girl's jeans are rolled up to her knees; her legs dangle over the edge of the boulder. Her sweater is buttoned up the front and a collar shows at her throat. Her hair, parted in the middle, is pulled tightly back. Her hands are folded in her lap. She looks as if she likes having a rock of her own to sit on.

On the back of the photograph, Kodak stamped the date of the print: October 3, 1955. Karen was born in 1947. I realized then what I was seeing. This child, with features barely preserved in faded pink, was Margie. Sitting there where the click of the shutter captured her image on film that day, she would live three more years before she disappeared from view. I looked out the windows into the yard. I looked at the wall where a calendar hung displaying a January that was sixty-seven years out of date. I looked at the faded image of the little girl sitting at the stream's edge, her hands folded on her lap. I knew then that this was Margie's room. She had come home. Through all these years she had remembered that safety was possible. She had found within these walls a place secured against the dangerous waters running close by.

TILT

*"We are, all of us,
at all times,
poised for
imminent fall."*

EMPTY FIELDS

E ven before I parked the jeep I could see that the field was empty. Still, I went through the motions, standing at the fence line, scanning the field with binoculars and then scanning it again with a spotting scope on the chance that somewhere in the acres of grain stubble stiffened under a cold November sky, I would detect the movement of horned larks. But the effort served only to confirm what I already knew–that there were no horned larks in this field or in any other field where they were accustomed to flock.

The absence of horned larks in the grass and sage habitat of eastern California, particularly in fall and winter when they gather by the thousands, is disorienting. Horned larks are normally so abundant that their presence frequently goes unnoticed. I have come back from birding these fields to find that the day's species list, meticulously recorded in my field book, lacked an entry for the horned lark although I had probably seen hundreds, if not thousands, of the species. Such absence of mind effectively defines one attribute of the familiar. But the most familiar is also the most pervasive and thus the most likely to assert its presence by change or disappearance. When I realized this year that the larks had disappeared, I felt their absence as some fundamental disorder, some distressing departure from the usual way of things.

My father died this winter in early December. And where I sat by him in his last moments, I saw the living presence in his eyes yield to absence, so that where there had been two of us an instant before, only one of us remained to count the loss.

Despite all the birds that have come to occupy their space, my mind still dwells on the absence of horned larks. When Mac McCormick called this winter to tell me he had discovered a rare mountain plover (the first ever reported in our area) in an eighty-acre field otherwise devoid of a single bird, anxious memory repopulated the field with a flock of four thousand horned larks he and I had come upon two winters ago. Shortly after Mac's call, when I went to see if I could confirm the sighting, the plover was gone, the field motionless and silent.

In late December our local Audubon group conducted its annual winter bird count. From daybreak to dark, teams of birders searched the fields for every individual bird of every species they could find. And when night overtook the effort and we gathered to total up the day's count, only one counter, Dave Shuford, could report a single horned lark. I took this as confirmation of loss, a last hard fact that no hope of mine could debate. Later, when I looked through Dave's written field report, I saw alongside this entry the notation "heard only." In an area that had recorded over six thousand horned larks in a day's count, we had come down to one thin call that had reached Dave on the still air of a December afternoon.

Had Dave seen as well as heard the horned lark, he would have seen its bright little forehead and face and throat of yellow; he would have seen the black bib and stripe below the eye and one black feather on each side of the crown like miniature horns; he would have seen it fly in short bursts that hugged the ground; and when it landed, he would have seen it like some feathered insect, sprinting in rasping jerks among the stubble. I have clung to Dave's report of that single call as to a ghost crying of continuity and possible return.

My father left his wife of sixty-six years, three children, seven grandchildren, and seventeen great-grandchildren. We gathered at his grave this winter to mourn the subtraction of one more from the count. Occasionally he calls to us across strangely altered fields of change, and our hearts flock momentarily to that voice of the familiar.

It is the inmost nature of Nature to change, and to change absolutely. Nothing can be held back, nothing kept, nothing saved. And however distressing this might seem to us, our survival lies in just such radical regeneration, the workings of which are a generosity beyond the count of loss or gain. We can only witness the disruption, accept its necessity, and listen for the voice of gratitude that whispers within.

BICYCLING

The absolute upright holds,
as it is, many phenomena
within its own delicate balance.

—Tozan Ryokai

THE MOST EXCELLENT MIRROR-SAMADHI

A bicycle is a vehicle consisting of a metal frame mounted on two wire-spoked wheels with rubber tires, a seat, handlebars for steering, and foot pedals for propelling it forward. It is often said of a bicycle that once you learn to ride one you never forget how. This claim is true enough but misleading in the way it is stated. The actual knowledge required to ride a bicycle is so elementary, so immediately and transparently obvious, that there is nothing that can be learned about riding one. You just get on, push off, pedal, and steer. Anyone can see how it's done. So it's nonsense to speak of learning how to ride a bicycle; one knows how to ride a bicycle before one has tried to do so.

But a bicycle is mounted on two wheels, not three. It is this feature that makes it possible to crash. It is also this feature that makes not crashing so indelible an accomplishment that one need never crash again. Resume bicycling in your mid-sixties, as I have recently done, and you will find that you don't crash. Yet the first time through, beginning with the afternoon Dad dropped the training wheels from your new Schwinn, you were taking out hedges and rearranging primroses in your mother's favorite flower bed and remodeling corners of the house until your elbows and knees were plastered over with the last of the Band-Aids in the medicine cabinet.

Then one day you managed the length of the driveway without mishap, and that was that. You never had to fear crashing again. Oh, you could run into things, or things could run into you, but the intrinsic certainty of crashing was put aside for good. So learning to ride a bicycle is not properly a matter of learning at all, but rather of getting the feel of the thing.

It turns out that the feel of the thing requires an exquisite sense of balance maintained by delicate and intricate mechanisms of instantaneous adjustment well beyond the scope of anything one could do on purpose. In riding a bicycle, one becomes an intuitive instrument of self-correction, sensing the exact and only point of equilibrium available in the instant, and doing so without benefit of decision. The feel of riding a bicycle is beyond the mechanics of choice.

I myself enact this ordinary little improbability almost daily now. My wife, Karen, and I recently moved from the Sierra Nevada Mountains to the town of Chico in California's Central Valley, where the land is flat and bicycling is a common means of getting about. We have bought a modest older house in a neighborhood known as "the avenues," where the pavement is canopied by the arching limbs of mature trees, and sidewalks are raised into little hills by the spread of their roots. We are at most ten bicycle minutes from the campus of California State University, about the same from Chico High School, Enloe Hospital, Bidwell Park, the Farmer's Market, and Cory's Restaurant in the center of town. Finding automobile parking at any of these destinations ranges from difficult to impossible, so nearly everyone in circumstances such as ours rides a bicycle.

With the car retired to the garage, my travels are more public now. Everything one does on a bicycle is done more openly than in a car. On a bicycle, no steel or glass wraps around you to divide your activities from the activities of others. No sounds or utterances of any sort are sealed either in or out. No carpeted floorboard disguises the pavement that rolls beneath your feet. No windshield turns away the weather. No independent suspension smoothes the ride. Bicycling is exposed and unavoidably social. On a bicycle, one confronts the world more nakedly, the whole sudden shifting immediacy of one's affairs opened out to the affairs of others.

Whatever you are by nature, whatever you have willed yourself to be, concentrates and distills itself on a bicycle: your timidities, your daring, your generosity or lack of it, your clumsiness or grace, whatever poise is naturally yours–all are telegraphed to others by the way you handle your bike. There's no effective rehearsal for a circumstance like this. What is needed is self-monitoring of a sort that lies outside anticipation and intent.

My favorite bicycle route takes me to the university library. Along the way I cross a narrow wooden bridge that spans Chico Creek on the edge of the campus. Not long after I had gotten my bicycle, I was entering this bridge from the north side of the creek just as a young woman on a bike, backpack over her shoulders and a stack of books bungied to the carrier, entered from the south side of the creek. There is just width enough on this bridge for two bicycles to pass one another, provided both riders stay alert and steady at the moment of passing. Following the custom of automobile travel, I inclined to my right. She simultaneously inclined to her left: thus we were opposed. I corrected to my left and she to her right; I again to my right, she left; whereupon we both hit the brakes and came to a standstill in the center of the bridge with our front wheels resting against each other's.

Her eyes flashed with irritation as she attempted to push her bike past me. I, concerned to clear a path for her, yanked my own bicycle aside and managed to block her way again. I was preparing phrases of apology when she turned to look at the creek where it flowed beneath our feet. And then she said to me quite matter-of-factly, "I'm so hurried these days I seldom stop to look at the water." In the midst of her vexation, she had restored balance and averted a crash. It was an instance of the most accomplished bicycling.

In December of our first year here in Chico, a heavy night storm swept through California's Central Valley. In the morning the soaking rains and high winds had toppled trees and dragged down power lines. Since Cory's Restaurant had power and we did not, Karen and I opted for breakfast out. In view of the weather, we took the car out of the garage and drove ourselves downtown where we found parking near enough to the restaurant that, with the aid of umbrellas, we got ourselves into Cory's in about as dry a condition as we could hope for.

Meanwhile, during a relative lull in the storm Professor Stillman, who teaches music at the university, walked to the music department to instruct his morning class. Under the scant protection afforded by the pink umbrella he habitually carries—woefully undersized for a man as tall as he—he managed to arrive fairly dry. But he arrived only to find the university without power and his class canceled.

Since Professor Stillman was already out and since he was to be deprived of the stimulation of teaching his class, he decided to head over to Cory's for some coffee and warmth. But on the way he was caught in a phenomenal cloudburst, which the wind drove in under that pitiful little umbrella, leaving him soaked to the skin from somewhere above his knees to the very undersides of his socks.

What I saw from where I sat at Cory's that morning was the sudden presence among the others waiting for a seat of a tall man in a tweed jacket folding down a miniature pastel-pink facsimile of an umbrella with the canopy ripped half off its ribbing. At the time I did not know that the person I saw was Professor Stillman or that he was a concert pianist or that his class had been canceled; nor did I know any of his other morning activities or thoughts. I was to learn these particulars a short time later in an extraordinary exchange of pleasantries.

Even from the distance of our table, I could see the extent of the soaking Professor Stillman had suffered during the assault of the storm. I recall feeling vaguely distressed by his condition. The fact of him standing there inside the door with his pants plastered to his legs weighed on me just enough that I could not fully enjoy my own favorable circumstances. He, on the other hand, seemed unnaturally disconnected from his situation, apparently perfectly poised, seemingly oblivious to the way in which others inclined away from him to avoid wetting their own garments. I studiously attended to my fruit dish in a vain effort to divert myself from the aggravating concern I felt for him. But any hope for success was dashed when the professor came sloshing after the hostess in shoes that had taken in so much water that he was wetly audible as he waded his way to a table not more than a yardstick's distance from mine and Karen's.

I witnessed then Professor Stillman's first and only concession to the discomforts of his situation. I saw him pluck at the fabric of his pants, squeezing up a bit of the soggy garment between his finger and thumb, and then I heard him complain in a remark directed only to himself, "I'm soaked." And that was that.

He then set out in a most detached and methodical manner to modify his circumstances as best he could. He removed his shoes one at a time and emptied the water from them. He took off his socks and wrung them as dry as he could. He carefully rolled up each pant leg, squeezing water from it as he went. He did these things with an exquisite precision of the sort one might associate with the performance of a difficult piano concerto, as though the process required the utmost of his talent and presence of mind. In the end, these improvements left him sitting clothed in nothing but his own damp skin from his knees to the floor, his bare feet resting in a puddle of his own making.

When Professor Stillman finished eating his heated muffin with sweet butter on the side and had settled into sipping his coffee, I engaged him in an exchange beginning (as if he didn't know!) with a comment on the extremity of the weather, something like, "This is some storm we're having." He acknowledged that it was and introduced himself. I asked how he'd managed to get caught in the downpour and he told me, but he quickly turned the conversation to our own recent arrival in Chico. He wondered if Karen and I found the community to our liking, and he told us some of the town's advantages and pleasures. He did this with such absorption in the details of our conversation that it was possible to forget I was talking to a man whose knees projected nakedly beyond the hem of the napkin he had unfolded on his lap.

For all his composure, it was evident that the professor could not help but know that his circumstance was exactly as it was and nothing other. I saw that his ease consisted not in having put his situation out of mind but in having fully included it, taking his wetness and nakedness upon himself in such a way that it did not tilt him from the absolute upright of the moment. As commonplace a social skill as this might be, Professor Stillman rode out the storm of these little morning miseries with the uncanny poise of a high-wire cyclist negotiating at each turn of the wheels the exact and only point of balance that would suffice.

I had seen Holly several times before the day of our first encounter. I had seen her helped to the car by her mother. I had watched her father carry her out to the yard to see the Christmas lights when she was too weak to get there on her own. I knew that she was only eleven years old, and that her blood circulated deadly leukemia cells that threatened to take her life, and that she was driven regularly to a San Francisco medical center where she underwent the most rigorous of chemotherapy schedules. I knew that she could no longer maintain her schooling and that, in dismay at what had become of her, she had told her mother that it wouldn't be so bad if she could just be "like the other kids for a while."

I first spoke to Holly at a neighborhood potluck to which Karen and I were invited so that we could meet our neighbors. Holly was having a strong day and had walked to the potluck with her mother's help from her own house two doors away. She sat in a lawn chair in the shade of a tree. She was utterly bald, her scalp like pale glass reflecting speckles of sunlight that sifted through the leaves. Her eyes looked remarkably large in a face grown thin with illness. Her whole head looked as if it might topple from its insubstantial neck. "I'm Lin," I said to her. "You must be Holly." "Hello," she said, and reached out a gaunt and trembling hand for me to shake.

We had been given name tags, and as I took Holly's hand, I saw what she had written on her tag. Pinned to her chest in dark bold letters was the name "Fuzzy." Looking down on her, I could catch a hint of my own reflection mirrored on the naked surface of her head. I found myself in a moment of gravest risk. I took a breath. Let it out. I looked her in the eyes and said, "I see I am in error and have mistaken you for Holly." "That's okay," she responded, "people often confuse me with Holly."

The disaster of her young life had taken away nearly all her options. But she held on to one of the few that was still hers and refused to be helpless. If she couldn't be like the other kids, like the kid she once was, then she would be exactly the kid she was now. And she would be this kid for all she was worth, wearing her baldness as though she had chosen it.

Behind this precarious play I saw a weariness that could topple this child off into a despair from which she might never right herself. Yet she had not toppled; she had intuited the need to tilt, sensing in that yielding and accommodating response some essential of her own survival. She had taken up the hand of death as a most unlikely playmate of her childhood and had tripped with it along the very edge of chance where the slightest misstep would surely bring a fall.

Bicycling incorporates tilt into balance. Unless one is willing to tilt toward a fall, one cannot avoid a fall. We are, all of us, at all times, poised for imminent fall. That we do not crash constantly is the working of a grace beyond our will. Do not think that we are held upright by the force of our own intent, for balance of itself seeks itself. We discard our training wheels when we acquire trust, when we discover that what is needed for our travels is already given to us in the very nature of things.

WINDOW BIRDS

In early October I crawled down off a ladder where I was caulking some siding on the house, doubled up with a pain that emanated from my lower back and traveled down my leg. I went into the house and lay down on the very bed where I now compose this writing.

Today is November 16, and with the exception of the most necessary movement inside the house and a few outings, such as being driven to therapy or to the Reno Diagnostic Center for an MRI or for consultation with a neurosurgeon, I have lain exactly here since I descended that ladder a month and a half ago.

From the bed where I lie, I look through windows that open to the southwest. I can see a forested ridge that rises from the grassy field where the house is situated. Today the ridge is shrouded in gray and snow blows through the trees. Gusts of cold wind shoulder against the house, causing the snow to whirl about the windows, and through this gauzy dimness I can see trees thrashing on the ridge above. I can see all this, lying on my back with my knees elevated to ease the pain that is perpetually with me. I can also see five little apple trees that my wife, Karen, and I planted, and the vegetable garden with its neat little plots all laid out and carefully fenced against the wind and the browsing deer.

It was on a day such as this a couple of weeks ago that the window birds came. Karen had gone to town for supplies, and I was alone in the house. It was about three in the afternoon, and the pain had come upon me in a hard way. I had taken a tablet of Vicodin, a narcotic prescribed for severe pain, and I was lying right here as I am now, trying to resist the futility of squirming about. I was exhausted. The best that could be said was that if hope had collapsed for a time, I was still holding on.

And then great tears formed, overran the sockets of my eyes, and spilled down the sides of my face. They did not feel like tears of my own making. They came as from the recesses of some common well of sorrow beyond the depths of any personal grief I might have known. They dropped silently. Through the smeared lenses of my eyes, beyond the window I could see the snow turn on the wind of a darkening sky.

Then there fluttered up into the window space, their wings brushing the very glass itself, the silhouettes of a small flock of sparrows. They seemed blown up against the window, carried like the snow on the force of the wind. They dropped out of sight beneath the level of the sill and rode up again into view. The wind swung them through the apple trees where they grabbed perches on the winter-bared limbs that pitched and shuddered beneath them. As they clung there for a second, I could make out the dark hoods of the juncos among them and the lateral crown stripes of a few white-crowned sparrows. There were perhaps a dozen of them gripping the tossing branches of the little trees, their feathers blown backward. Then as one they all let go and disappeared in the darkness up the ridge.

But even before the little flock was lost to sight, while I could still see them bobbing in the wind as they receded in the distance, I recognized that joy had come. Before this recognition, before it had been framed as thought, I knew that I had simply become joy, the whole of me, without reservation, without anything set aside. I felt joy not in addition to or in spite of my circumstances, but rather the whole of my circumstances had simply *become* joy.

Joy is an act of love. My eyes loved the little birds and the wind and the trees; the tears that blurred these same eyes loved the birds and the wind and the trees; the wet skin of my face loved them; the breath that moved in me loved them; my whole body where it lay injured with its useless legs propped up on pillows loved them; the very pain itself where it rolled out in waves from my injured spine loved the little birds and the wind and the trees.

The window birds are memory now. Beyond the window, I see the garden buried in snow. Down under, the garden lies fallow and waits, as I lie here fallow and wait, as everywhere, in all places, at all times, and in all beings, joy lies fallow and waits.

OUR ONLY NAME

*"And every sound served
to call me back to myself,
until the whole barn
resounded with my name."*

THE EGG BARN

Each mortal thing does
one thing and the same:
Deals out that being
indoors each one dwells;
Selves—goes itself;
myself it speaks and spells,
Crying What I do is me:
for that I came.
—Gerard Manley Hopkins, *KINGFISHERS*

T he egg barn was little more than a shed really, about the size of a garage. It stood on the outermost perimeter of a 360-acre farm located in a remote area of the Irvine Hills of southern California. The farm was my father's, and he had leased the acreage to raise turkeys. In addition to the egg barn, the farm also had a feed barn, stalls for two work horses, a small house and yard, a well, and thousands of feet of poultry fencing strung on metal T-posts to form enclosures for a hundred thousand turkeys.

None of these other structures could be seen from the egg barn, which stood down a long hill on the edge of a wash. The wash itself was a narrow crease of moist earth where a few willows survived. In the early mornings or late evenings when the turkeys were restless, one could hear them from the egg barn, their cackling faint in the distance, the smell of them on the wind. But all one could see of the rest of the farm were tire tracks disappearing in the weeds up slope.

As a boy, I worked long hours in the egg barn. I lost my childhood to such work. In time I nearly lost myself as well. To understand why this happened, one must know how I was first put to work and what the nature of that work was.

My brother, Rowland, and I began working on the farm when we were still very young. As far back as I can remember I had to rush home from school to do chores; but the summer Rowland was ten and I was eight, Father put us to work full time. We were to get a week's vacation before school resumed in the fall. It was time, he told us, to learn what a day's work was. My mother supported Father in this new regimen, seeing to it that Rowland and I were on the job by seven and that we did not overstay the lunch hour.

I received this like a punishment, as though I had been put to these labors as a penance for some wrong. I wanted to ask what it was that I had done, but my father's strange sternness regarding the matter silenced me. From the hot summer fields where I chopped weeds or rolled up poultry fencing, I could see the laundry drying in the shade near the house, and I yearned for the cool return to a refuge from which I felt exiled.

The whole of that summer passed in tight little increments like the staccato advance of the second hand round the face of a clock. It was the longest ninety days of my life, yet it was not time enough to make right again whatever it weeds. I took each egg in hand, one at a time, and if even the faintest manure stain was found on it or a smear of blood from a hen's egg tract, I scoured it clean with sandpaper. Father had warned me that the slightest impurity that found its way into the incubator could sicken a whole hatch of chicks. When I was sure the eggs were clean, I put them into the incubators from where, after a few weeks, I took them out again to be candled. This involves putting a light to the egg in a darkened room so that the inside of the egg is illuminated and one can see the developing embryos. In the living eggs, I could make out the form of a tiny chick taking shape around its own beating heart. In others, I saw only the shadow of a lifeless yolk rotting in the warmth of the incubator. In the egg barn with the window shades drawn and incubators humming in darkness against the wall, I put the candling light to each egg, discarding the failures in a garbage pail that waited beside my stool.

I worked alone those days, and while I had no yearning for company, the solitude wore away at me. I stood by the table in the egg barn and sanded eggs until my hands and forearms, and even my hair and face, and the table itself were coated with chalky dust. I breathed egg shell and manure and traces of turkey blood. I felt increasingly vague, as indeterminate as the accumulating days and weeks I spent working there. Hour after hour I moved among the crates of eggs like a prisoner in solitary confinement who, when sentenced to the presence of his own person, finds himself locked up with a stranger. Under the unrelieved scrutiny of my own attention, I turned myself round and round in my mind like some unformed embryo that had failed to incubate and had so irretrievably lost the source of its own becoming that it was utterly unfamiliar to itself. Outside, the wind blew across the fields of dust and feathers and withered weeds. Sand scraped against the barn's corrugated metal sides.

Once in a while Al or Hector or one of the other farm hands would come down to the egg barn to put in a spare hour helping me. They too were becoming like strangers to me. They might pull their hats off where the sweatband had left a hot crease across their foreheads. They might wipe the grit and sweat from themselves with a handkerchief or a rag. They might complain about the heat or about the farm truck whose battery was failing. They might tease me about the Stillford girl who lived on a neighboring farm and whom they liked to imagine I had a crush on, but none of this penetrated the odd detachment that grew on me during the long hours I spent alone. I could find nothing of myself clarified in their company. I bore no necessary relationship to them—nor to anyone else for that matter, not even my father whose visits to the egg barn were rare. He always formalized them into employer/employee encounters, a stiffness that only magnified the absence I felt in his presence there.

And then one hot summer afternoon in my fourteenth year, six years after my father had first set me to work, he came to the egg barn to count the eggs we had in stock. As he left he did something unusual. He put his hand on my shoulder and gave a little squeeze, and said, "How's the young working man doing?" He stood there as if he were actually waiting for an answer, and he didn't take his hand away. I put my own hand over his and held it fast to my shoulder. And then I saw, in just the merest flicker of his eyes, that my father could not tell me who I was because he himself did not know. I was as much a stranger to him as he was to me. We were both made momentarily awkward by the unspoken disclosure of this fact in one another's faces. Father turned away first and went out the door, saying something about egg production being slightly improved over the previous month.

I heard him start the engine of his car and then I heard the sound of it recede into the distance. I went outside in time to see him disappear over the rise that separated the egg barn from the rest of the farm.

In the egg barn, I took up my work again. Down in the wash the willows shimmered in waves of heat. Then I was going toward the wash, down through the brittle stalks of weeds, the foxtails pricking me where they stuck to my socks. Under the willows, the sand was smooth and cool. I lay myself there face down. It was not enough. I took my shirt off. Still, it was not enough. I pulled off my shoes and socks and stripped away the last of my clothing and pressed the whole of my naked body onto the ground. I dug a little concave in the moist sand, and I lowered my eyes and mouth into this space. And there, where the willows had found water, I breathed into the earth.

My name is Lin. I am fourteen years old. I am lying right here on the ground under the willows, in the wash beyond the egg barn on my father's farm.

When I knew these things for certain, I dressed and

went back to my work. In the silence of the barn the sound of my work seemed amplified. The drag of an egg crate on the work table, the thin scratch of sandpaper, the scrape of a footstep or the whisper of my breath—each was clarified and insistent. And every sound served to call me back to myself until the whole barn resounded with my name. Was it Father who called from where he sat at the farm office desk, his eyes blinking behind his glasses, his fingers pressing a sharpened pencil onto the columns of an egg ledger? Was it Rowland calling from where he scooped grain into the turkey feeders, his back bending again and again to the task, his face wet with sweat? Did my mother call from the car where she turned onto the county road toward Schneider's grocery? Were Al and Hector calling from the fields? Had they set aside their tools and turned their faces toward the hill that hid me from their view and called my name? There in the egg barn I looked out on the wash where the sand still held the impression of my body. Weren't we all of us pressed to earth, here, in this field, of one voice, calling our only name?

VESTMENTS

*The sage will tell a trainee
who is feeling he is low
and all inferior that on his head
there gleams a jeweled diadem,
and on his body rich robes hang,
and at his feet there is a footrest.*
—Tozan Ryokai,
THE MOST EXCELLENT MIRROR-SAMADHI

Aside from those attached to my car, I own two mirrors. One hangs by the bathroom sink, a mirror just large enough to give me the image of my face and hair. The other is a full-length mirror stored in the back of a bedroom closet. I have recently hauled this mirror out and propped it against the bedroom wall where I can look at myself in new clothes I have bought. I notice their color and texture and fit. This is behavior unprecedented in the sixty-three years of my life.

In the past I can recall nothing beyond an almost studied indifference to anything other than the utility of what I wore. My clothes had to be practical, durable, and cheap. Once purchased, they had to be faithfully cared for and made to last as long as possible. I would no more think of discarding a usable garment for its lack of current stylishness than I would think of throwing away a shovel or hammer that still had some work left in it. I acquired these virtues as a child growing up in the household of a Danish immigrant father who had come to this country with an eighth-grade education, no money, and little English, and who found himself a few years later struggling to raise a family and get ahead in the wake of the nation's worst economic depression.

As a child, I watched my father go off in the dark of the morning wearing the stiff gray work shirt and pants issued him by the gas company and carrying a lunch pail with his name scratched on it. I watched his return in the evening, after which he worked until bedtime trying to make our small farm pay off. My brother and I were barely school age when we were put to the service of these needs, forfeiting nearly all our spare time to the chores required of the place. I went to these chores with a fearful urgency born of my father's struggle, and I longed, as only such a child can, to sacrifice something on his behalf.

In those days, my father and mother and my brother and I—even my baby sister, Evelyn—seemed to live out our precarious lives in deadly earnest. My father, whose fragile pride required some defense on his part, scorned those who had not found employment on the merit of their own efforts and had to settle for jobs with the National Public Works Project. "Make-work," he called it. But when the gas company laid off his entire crew, my father too had to accept help from the project. He no longer had work clothes issued to him, and he sometimes had to go to work in old Sunday clothes that had become too frayed to wear "for good."

I suspect my parents initially put my brother and me into jeans because jeans were durable and could be bought a size too large and still last long enough to be grown into before they wore out. Along with a few simple shirts and a jacket, these jeans constituted our school clothes. When they became too frayed for school we wore them for work. Each of us, my parents included, had one outfit that we wore only for church or other dress-up occasions. Otherwise, our good clothes hung in the closet safe from wear or harm. The necessities that drove my family to these frugal measures ended long ago, but my behavior did not. I continued to wear jeans unless circumstances required something else. I never regarded my own clothing as a source of pleasure or beauty. I carried austerity into all my doings, a certain strain of renunciation that seemed to come quite naturally to me. As an adult I took lay ordination as a Soto Zen Buddhist, drawn to the simple and unadorned practices of the Buddhist monks.

But this has changed now, and the change came about in this way: I recently injured my spine and underwent surgery to mitigate pain and dysfunction. After surgery, during the period of earliest rehabilitation, I found that my jeans were too binding, causing pain and restricting movement. I needed to find something else to wear. For the first time in memory, I went to a clothing store to buy clothes other than what I had always bought. What I found was a pair of tightly woven, sandwashed khaki cotton pants. In the dressing room, I unbuttoned my jeans and slid them off and hung them aside on a peg. I pulled on the new pants. They felt and looked unfamiliar. The fabric lay smoother against my skin. The cut was roomier so that the garment felt almost airy in its lightness. There were cuffs and pleats that spread when I pushed my hands into the pockets. But they were comfortable, and in some undefinable way, the image reflecting from the dressing-room mirror pleased me. I took the pants home, and that was the beginning.

Since then I have bought three more pairs of pants, some T-shirts in soft colors with a pocket on the front, a cotton seersucker shirt in a pattern of thin alternating stripes of green and bone, a short-sleeved cotton shirt of tan, and a dozen pairs of socks in tones of earthen green and light brown. I like wearing these things, and I have recently found myself recalling with pleasure the remarkably beautiful robes the Buddhist monks sometimes wear for special ceremonial occasions.

Sometimes when I prop the mirror against the bedroom wall and look at myself in my new pants and, perhaps, the green T-shirt with a pocket on the front, the eyes in the mirror seem to reflect a little surprise, a little wonder at what they see there. At such times some unexplained tenderness, some melancholy, some softly rising joy comes to me. I was puzzled by this until on one such occasion I recalled the time of my father's new suits.

By 1945, the farm was finally paying enough that my father no longer had to work a second job. In fact, earnings from the farm had reached a little beyond absolute need. For the first time since immigrating in 1928, he had a small surplus at his discretion. He spent some of the money to have two suits custom tailored for him. The social circumstances of this tailoring was an issue of some delicacy to my father for reasons that I must explain.

My father had a deformity on his back in the form of a hump that bulged out on one side in the area of his shoulder blade. This defect was not terribly severe but certainly noticeable enough to draw a child's attention and elicit questions. But any such curiosities were apparently intercepted by my mother while I was still very young. She expressly forbade us children to ever speak of it to our father. She gave only the vaguest intimations of early injury or sickness in explanation of the deformity. Then we were instructed to put it out of mind and out of speech. Being thus enjoined to silence on the matter, this unspoken dialogue between my father and me became for a time our most persistent conversation, the language of an obvious and awkward avoidance audible in all we said.

I was always intensely aware of any circumstances pertaining to what I had come to designate as "Father's back." If he took pain medication for his back, I knew of it. If he undertook any physical therapy or received chiropractic intervention or took heat treatments, I knew of it. In the same manner I somehow learned that my father's new suits were to be custom fitted to accommodate the hump on his back. For the first time in his life, he would have a jacket that hung properly. Though only twelve at the time, I understood the significance of this. His tailor, I learned, was an acquaintance who had also immigrated to this country and with whom my father felt comfortable. I understood the point of this as well. It must have seemed to me as if everyone I knew was conspiring to guard this most public of secrets.

The formal declaration of these undertakings came one night at the supper table. Whenever Father had something really important to announce, such as the birth or marriage or death of one of our distant Danish relatives, he would stop eating, lay whatever utensils he happened to be using at the side of the plate, fold his hands in his lap, and look out on the rest of us in an attitude of expectation. Since he would do this in the midst of eating his meal, it would naturally draw our attention and signal to us that an announcement of some sort was imminent. We would all look at him and wait until he was assured of our full attention, and then he would deliver his announcement.

On this particular night, he proceeded to tell us something to the effect that the ranch had done very well that year and had cleared over twelve thousand dollars. We would be buying some things we needed, but we couldn't buy whatever we wanted because, if we weren't careful, he could find himself out "carrying a lunch pail again." And then he added, "I am having George Wanger cut me two dress suits. They will be made of the finest material money can buy." This done, Father resumed his meal. And though none of us pursued this subject any further, I remember being pretty impressed with the event, as if I had been present at an important public function.

During the next several weeks, I was aware that my father went regularly to the tailor's shop for fittings. I could not prevent myself from trying to imagine how George

Wanger could get the cloth to fit properly to Father's back. I imagined him stretching the material to form a sort of accommodating bulge or stitching in extra material where it was needed. I was driven to these speculations by the heartfelt wish that Father's suits would turn out right and by the fear that they would not. I had come to think of my father's deformity as a sort of painful disease, bad enough that it mustn't be spoken of, and from which he could never be cured. I earnestly hoped that the suits would somehow help to make my father okay again, the way he must have been before whatever it was that had happened. My fantasies of tailoring were prayers for his healing.

The suits came home without my ever knowing of it, so I was quite surprised when my father gathered up my brother and me shortly after lunch one day and told us, "I have something to show you boys." He led us into his and Mother's bedroom, an act which in itself was unusual because it was somehow understood that we boys were to stay out of there. He pulled open the closet door and stood aside, inviting us without a word to look within.

There were the suits. They were unlike any other articles of clothing that hung among my father's things. One was dark, a blended wool of rich browns; the other was light, a blended gray with closely spaced darker threads running through it. They were both double-breasted and had wide lapels. Father took each in turn from the closet and laid it on the bed so that we could better see the front with its pocket and the lining, which he exposed for us, and the startling inside pocket, a feature I had no idea even existed. He showed us the trousers with pleats and cuffs.

And then he held the suits up by their hangers, one in each hand. With the air of one who is disclosing a confidentiality of the most serious kind, he said, "These suits are made of the finest material money can buy." I had a habit in those days of whistling tunes a lot, particularly when I worked. All that afternoon while I went about my farm chores, I kept whistling, feeling that now things would be okay.

In the following year the ranch continued to prosper. Father began to do things he had never done before, and he did most of them in his new suits. He and my mother took lessons in ballroom dancing from Carla Wanger, the tailor's wife. When they had learned a new dance, they went to Vivian Laird's, a dine-and-dance club all the way over in Long Beach, thirty miles away, to try out what they had learned. They looked grand to me going out the door together, Father in one of his new suits (he was quite whimsical about which one he might on any occasion choose to wear) and Mother in a slinky mauve gown with a matching jacket she could discard when they took to the dance floor. Father seemed to love wearing his suits, and he would sometimes dress up just to go to a dance lesson or to do some banking or other casual thing. I recall him on one occasion driving away in our old Hudson sedan, wearing his gray suit with a handkerchief folded in the pocket, on his way to the dentist to have his teeth cleaned.

In those wonderful days of my father's new suits, I felt safer than I had ever before felt as a child. And the safest place of all was at Sunday service in Trinity Episcopal Church where my father had begun to serve as an usher. He greeted the other members as they arrived and showed them to their seats, helping some to remove their overcoats and hanging them in the cloak room. Best of all, he distributed and collected the offering plates during the service. I felt then, sitting in a pew beside my brother and sister and mother, that some mournful curse had at last been lifted from my father's back, that we were all rich, and that Father would never have to carry a lunch pail again.

And he never did. Yet in the course of a few years, my father quit his new church functions and withdrew once more into the guarded privacy of his past behaviors, devoting his energies almost exclusively to keeping the ranch solvent. "One really bad year could wipe me out and I could lose everything," he would sometimes say. His suits hung idle in the bedroom closet. In his last years, finding it harder and harder to dress at all, he spent his days in the same pajamas in which he eventually died.

Nevertheless, in this moment of my own awakening, the resurrected father in his marvelous new suit, his face as serious as if our collective salvation had been put in his hands, carries the offering plate up the aisle to the very altar itself. It is received by Reverend Hailwood, who lifts the plate up, up, upward, and we all rise and sing the doxology, and my father is still there—there where the whole congregation can acknowledge the importance of what he has just done, there at the very front of the church.

Oh, Father, is it not strange that after all the frugal self-discipline and denial, after all the secrecy and fear, we are drawn now toward one another as much by our minor self-indulgences and the small amenities we have allowed ourselves as ever we were by our shared sacrifices? Here before this mirror, searching the image of myself dressed in my new khakis with their pleats and cuffs and neat creases pressed down the front of each leg, and with the soft blue T-shirt with its single pocket, I wonder, Father, what it is that we have wanted to be and seldom had the courage to become? Let these—my new clothes and your two suits of the finest material money can buy—let these be the ritual vestments of our becoming what we are.

In a monastery outside Mount Shasta, California, I watch a group of Soto monks gather in the temple. There are forty of them, all clothed in dark robes draped with ritual cloths of deepest purple and saffron. They approach the altar where they form themselves in four equal lines facing the figure of the Buddha. Their movements are measured and exact as they unfold their kneeling cloths, forty squares of embroidered white silk drawn off their shoulders and spread on the floor before them. The temple gong sounds. The monks drop to their knees and, in a movement as sudden and delicate as the beat of a moth's wings, arch forward to touch their foreheads to the floor, the purple and saffron of their vestments fluttering and settling over the squares of silk like brilliant insects drawn to white blossoms. It is an homage paid in beauty to the source of beauty before the altar of its being. It is the chrysalis unfolding to the light of its own awakening. It is the bright face of mutual recognition reflecting itself in the image of its own true nature.

I SPEAK FOR
MY FATHER

My father lived and died without speaking for himself. His thoughts and feelings were sometimes conveyed to me by my mother but, aside from matters of common utility, I got little from him directly. I say now for him what he did not say for himself. I have set myself to do this because I need to know what shape my father takes when put to words. Should I, from the grave of his long silence, unearth some remnant of his unspoken mind, I will surely bring to light something of my own. If I falter along the way, it is because I reconstruct my father's voice from the most disparate of sources and because his language is new to me.

Harslev, Denmark, 1916. The Percheron stallion shows dark against the horizon, its coat of blue-black darker even than the rich earth curling off the shearing edge of the plow. The plow strains against the resisting soil, but the Percheron moves forward with a containment and strength that never breaks stride. There where the field slopes down to the shore, an evening light streams in across the North

Sea, painting the water silver and reflecting off the rippling muscles of the great draft animal.

My father, small and slim, only a boy of seventeen years, follows the plow—not, as so many do, stumbling along in the furrow, yanking at the plow handles and grabbing at the reins to bring the horse back on line. My father follows on the unturned edge, one easy hand teasing the plow to its proper depth, the reins resting lightly on his shoulders, his free hand gently telegraphing its message along the length of the reins, telling the Percheron what is required of him. His control of the animal is exquisite.

My father, who has hired out to work a neighbor's fields, is the youngest of the hands on Jens Pederson's farm. Yet he alone works the stallion. The morning my father came down from Eilskov, Jens Pederson led the animal from its stall and put the halter rope into my father's hands. "This is the best I have ever owned," he told him. "He needs to learn harness. Were your father able, Jochum Christian is the only one I'd trust the animal to. Since he is not, I trust his son." And so my father brings the big stallion down the day's last pass of the field toward the sea, the Percheron pressing itself against the hames, the traces drawn tight, my father guiding the bite of the plow so that nothing goes slack. Beyond the field, the surf runs with the tide up the shallow rise of the sea's edge.

At the foot of the field, my father tilts the plow out of its furrow and brings the stallion to rest. He unbuckles the traces and secures them to the hames for the return to the barn. But then he pauses, his eyes searching the sea, his hand resting on the animal's flank. He has decided what he is going to do. He drags the harness from the stallion's back and hangs it over the handles of the resting plow. He takes up the reins and starts the Percheron down to the water.

The Percheron strides onto the slaty gray stones of the beach with my father trotting after. Flocks of gulls scatter and wheel overhead, their cries riding away on the breeze. The Percheron reaches the water, hesitating, its knees lifting high. For an instant, Father fears it will not go on. Then a ripple of gathering strength runs through the haunches of the great animal and it plunges forward, legs pumping against the pull of the surf, the salt spray staining its coat even darker. Father knows now that the stallion will go all the way.

The long shallow slope of the beach gradually deepens, the Percheron parting the incoming waves. Father crowds in behind it to escape the drag of the water. Still he goes on. He does this for the boy he once was who, at seven years, stood with his younger sister, Annette, and his younger brother, Acten, and his older brother, Johannes, and his eldest brother, Julius, the firstborn, in the courtyard of the Eilskov farm where the women had told them to stand. He drives now deeper into the sea for this boy who watched when the men came from the isolation hospital dressed in white coats buttoned tightly at the throat and wrist, with white gloves and gauze masks concealing their faces under heads bound tight in cloth. He does this for the boy whose mother was taken from her bed and carried past him to the waiting wagon as she lay on the stretcher, her face turned toward him where he stood with his brothers and sister, her large, soft eyes searching her children's faces. He urges the great stallion on now for the boy who saw in his mother's eyes a presence that frightened him and who started toward her but was pulled away by the women just as he heard his mother's sharp command, "Stay back!" He goes deeper now for the boy whose father hid in the house until it was too late and the hospital wagon had disappeared in the mist beyond the hedge.

And my father goes on for the boy of fourteen years he once was whose father lost his mind to a stroke, his eyes gone crazed, his high, pale forehead twisted by paralysis, all his beautiful, articulate speech turned to gurgling incoherence. He goes on for the boy whose father shivered and drooled and coughed up whatever he was fed and whose once gifted hands, which coaxed to harness the most willful horse, fidgeted uselessly now at the bed covers, but who still could not die.

And most of all, he goes on for the boy of seventeen who, night after night, hearing his father cry out in startled madness, held him to his bed so that he would not go raging about on his knees in the darkened bedroom. He does this for the boy who, fearing the loss of his own mind, begged his brother, Julius, to take over for him, that he couldn't bear it anymore. He goes on for the boy who, broken and disappointed in himself, ashamed that he had abandoned his father's need, retreated to the farm of Jens Pederson where he took up the reins of the great Percheron stallion.

My father, following the Percheron, is nearly afloat now. He threads the fingers of one hand through the coarse hairs of its tail, leaving his other free to manage the reins.

He can go perhaps a hundred yards more before the beach drops out from under the horse, leaving it awash in the surf. At any moment, the animal could drop into a depression and be lost. My father knows that he could not face Jens Pederson alive if this were to happen. But the Percheron churns on into ever deepening water, the surf breaking over its back now, my father taking the animal to the absolute edge of his capacity to control it.

And then it steps off the ledge and plunges beneath the water. My father is dragged under, the reins stripped from his hand. He holds on by the base of the Percheron's tail and draws himself onto its back until he can reach the mane. He feels the powerful muscles of the stallion still driving its legs, frantically seeking a firmness underfoot that will move it forward. My father has gone beyond all rules, all rehearsal, all practiced elements of control. He needs his father's gift now as he has never needed it before. Knowing this, my father suspends all judgment and, reaching beyond anything he knows to do, he wills the Percheron to calmness, until it gradually stops thrashing and rises to the surface. The animal's legs slowly revolve, suspended in water, its great bulk inching forward until at last the hooves make contact. Father retrieves the reins and turns the horse toward shore.

Harslev, Denmark, 1919. In summer, the young people hear the music drifting across the fields from the pavilion above the town pond. The women have already ironed their dresses and bathed themselves, and now they hurry the supper things off the table, the foods returned to the cooler, the plates and utensils scoured and dried and stacked on cupboard shelves. The men too have bathed before eating. They have brushed down their best pants and jackets, and now they make the last rounds of the stock and go to dress themselves.

The music is lively and the dancers whirl, their motions duplicated in shadows the pavilion lights cast on the surface of the pond. My father has become very popular and he dances nearly every dance. He wears a tie and keeps his jacket neatly buttoned throughout the whole of the evening, not stripping it off to dance in shirt and loosened tie as some others do. His hair is rich auburn and lies in waves, his forehead smooth, broad. Some sort of dark knowledge shows in his eyes, which is at once troubling and attractive to the women. His mouth is full and sensual. The young women put themselves in his way by design, hoping he will ask them to dance. If he doesn't, they sometimes ask on their own behalf. A few have seen him in the fields stripped to the waist, his body lean and muscular, the big stallion moving easily under his command. At twenty, my father is a good prospect for marriage. Some of the women view him in this way. Others simply want to feel his arms about them.

My father is only vaguely aware of his attractiveness. His mother gone so early, he has learned little about women. Outside the work of the fields, he has felt mostly uncertainty and shyness. How to talk to a woman, how to walk with her or dance or ask for what you want from her—all this is beyond my father's knowing. But Jens Pederson's wife has made him shirts, and Jens Pederson himself has sent to Odense for proper dress clothes. The young women—Pederson's own domestic help and daughters from neighboring farms—have coaxed my father out of his shyness. His dancing is not polished. When he takes the women in his arms, his lead is more an insistence than a request. He feels a certain mastery in this. He feels wonderful.

Harslev, Denmark, 1920. Lying on the cot in the darkened stable room, my father has no clear hopes or fears. He has only pain. He has lain here, fevered and delirious, until time is only a vague uncertainty. He remembers everything up to that exact moment in the loft when he felt something give way in him—the shortness of breath, the dizziness, the gradual onset of weakness, the will it took to finish a day's work, his refusal to speak of these things. He remembers the bale being passed up to him. He remembers taking its weight and shifting it onto his knees, burying the hooks and swinging it up, the force of his body behind the lift. And then he remembers only pain, the hot shock of it beneath his shoulder blade.

Afterwards, pain was all there was—the lantern hanging from the stable room rafters, my father's eyes swimming up into the dim glow of it, the women wiping sweat from his eyes, the gasps that escaped him from the sheer pain of breathing. He does not remember the fever that came as a blessing to blot out his mind. Nor does he remember the light that came and went from the stable room window in the days that followed, nor the ice that was packed around him, nor the bed clothing that was stripped and freshened daily, nor even the broth that was spooned into him when one of the women propped him up while another tilted his head back to get him to swallow.

He remembers finding himself here in the night, a gradual and dim awakening. He remembers rolling onto his stomach, his face pushed into the cot, straining to get his arm over his shoulder, reaching for the source of his pain, his fingers tracing the contour of what he discovers there, the full extent of his deformity, the awful ruin of it, his hand clamped hard over his mouth, his own father's agonies piercing his ears. Afterwards, he cannot tolerate the sunshine and asks that the window be covered.

In the kitchen and in the milk barn, the young women whisper of my father as of one dead; they speak pity and loss that such a young beauty has been brought down. My father, lying in the darkened room, has made a decision. His own father, forever blighted and wasting away, shall surely die soon, and Julius, the eldest son, will inherit the Eilskov farm. There is no future here. If my father heals enough to work again, he will save his earnings and emigrate to the United States.

Orange, California, 1927. My father is having his picture taken. He has bought himself a car. The car has a retractable cloth top and full seats, front and back. He has already met Lucy Goslee, and the car is big enough to take her and her parents or her friends wherever they want to go. He poses for the picture in a suit and tie with a dark overcoat. He stands by the car, one hand resting on the window ledge, declaring his ownership. With the other arm, elbow cocked out, he holds a dress hat to his side. He has already secured his citizenship and has steady employment caring for a local orchard. He feels prosperous and looks directly into the lens.

Laguna Beach, California, May 1, 1928. My father walks on the beach below the lighted windows. It is his wedding night in the little hotel on the cliffs that Lucy chose. It has cost them a lot of money and their stay will be short. They are both virgins, and my father is gripped by sudden uncertainty. My mother has never even seen him with his shirt off and, though he has spoken briefly of its existence, he has never exposed for her the hump that projects from his back. He paces back and forth now, glancing repeatedly at the windows. In the room with the elegant curtains, where yellow roses repeat themselves in the dressing table mirror, my mother waits. She is not yet eighteen and has no experience to guide her. Yet, when my father returns, she will behave as if he had only gone out for a casual smoke and some air, and though she aches for him to have what she offers, she will bring him to it as gently as she can.

Later, lying warmed and delighted with what they have done, they touch each other everywhere and he tells her she is not Lucy Goslee anymore, but Lucy Jensen. They do not know they have wed on the eve of the century's worst depression.

Orange, California, 1934. My father is indignant that my mother and Dr. Robbins refer to his condition as a "nervous breakdown." His back hurts him and he can't sleep nights. He's just tired, he tells himself. People with nervous breakdowns end up in the county mental hospital. Is that where they think he belongs? Then who will put food on the table? He hasn't time for a breakdown.

He watches Mother now as she clears away the dishes. It's Sunday noon after church. Father sits in his dress pants and white shirt at the head of the table. Mother has baked a cake and Rowland, my brother, has been told he can't have any until he finishes his vegetables. He picks desultorily at some cooked carrots, his chubby fingers separating them from the onions, which he hates. I, Linley, sit in an infant chair pulled up to the table. I am towheaded and my teeth are bucked, pushing my upper lip out. Mother moves back and forth from the kitchen. She wears a summer dress and an apron pulled snug at her waist. She lifts her hair from her neck to cool herself. Father's mood is softened by this. He thinks she is beautiful. He wishes he had her alone to himself. He wishes he felt better.

Later, Father will change into work clothes and go into the back yard to clean the coops and feed the small flock of turkeys he is raising there. His neighbors think this a nuisance and complain of the noise and smell. But Father thinks he can make some money this way. In time, he thinks, he can lease some acreage and expand his flock. He would like to buy Mother something nice.

Garden Grove, California, 1940. My father has received word of the death of his brother Acten, found hung by his own belt from the rafters of an outhouse. With his brother

Johannes already dead before age forty from a heart attack, Father has only Annette and Julius left. He will not talk about Acten's suicide.

Mother has given birth to my sister, Evelyn, who, six years after my own birth, was not intended. The delivery, difficult and prolonged, has left Mother badly shaken. She suffers frequently from what she calls "sick" headaches and goes to bed claiming she is ill. She complains that she can't control Rowland and me. "They're out of hand. You have to do something," Mother insists. He does something. He orders them one at a time to strip and lie face down on the upstairs bed. He flails away at them with a lath stick, beats, once and for all, some lasting order into his life.

Later from behind his newspaper, he sees Rowland come down the stairs and go into the kitchen. But I am the son who crawls up on his lap insisting on how sorry I am. And neither father nor son have any idea what the son is supposed to be sorry for. My father is fearful of his son's softness, his easy tears, his unguarded capitulation, his hunger that love be made known. It bends him in places he thinks ought to remain straight. This son of his exposes an injury in him like that of the hump on his back of which he never speaks and of which his sons never speak because their mother has forbidden them to do so.

Awakening in the night, he hears my mother crying in an adjacent room. He is certain she wants him to hear her. For a moment, he pities and forgives her this weakness. But his own, old night dread stiffens him and prevents him from going to her. "Come to bed, Lucy," he calls, hearing a sharpness in his voice he had not intended.

Santa Ana, California, 1964. My father sits in the farm office, a lined and columned financial ledger opened on the desk before him. To his left are a pad and sharpened pencils lined up in readiness for his use. To his right is a calculating machine with numbered keys and a handle that cranks out the tape. He wears glasses and holds a fountain pen for making finished entries in the ledger. The ledger documents three consecutive years of heavy losses.

Rowland, whom he has kept home, will have no farm to inherit. It angers my father that he can do nothing to make the outcome otherwise. He is glad I have found a place elsewhere teaching at a central California college. He imagines me among those books he so often saw me read when I was still a child. He wonders what it is that his wife and son talk about when I come to visit. He thinks of Evelyn, married now, she and her young husband already wealthy from real estate investment. Perhaps he has been too cautious? He remembers the Percheron powering its way into the surf. He remembers the women, turning flushed and young in his arms at the pavilion above the pond. He remembers the car in which he drove Lucy Goslee to the movies. He cannot believe it all ends in a ledger page that won't balance.

He locks the door to the office and goes into the house to ask my mother something he has not asked her in years. He finds her in bed. She is not feeling well and thinks she should lie down for a while. He asks her anyway. He asks her if she'd like to drive over to Long Beach to Vivian Laird's, a dine-and-dance restaurant overlooking the beach. "We could have supper and dance." She asks if she can take a rain check.

Orange, California, Spring 1993. Gradually this house of his retirement has taken my father prisoner. He has lost the will and the strength to leave it. He relies on my mother to help him through the day. He sleeps most of the time. He is ashamed of this and tells Rowland that this is "no way for a man to live." None of us knows the extent of the cancer that eats his body away and makes his least effort heroic.

He grieves now the loss of Acten, dead by his own hand. He grieves the loss of Johannes and of Annette, who, wandering the wards of a Copenhagen rest home, has forgotten who she is. He grieves the loss of Julius, dead three years now. He grieves the loss of the Eilskov farm, gone to heirs that are strangers to him.

He tells Evelyn that he needs to die. He wants her help. She tells him she can't help him that way. He asks her to draw the curtains because the light hurts his eyes. But in the darkened room he sees once more the long night of his father's eyes, vacant of any mind a son might recognize. He sees his mother, carried helpless and doomed, beyond his reach, to the waiting wagon.

Tustin, California, December 8, 1993. The nurses, alerted by the monitor, converge on my father's bed to confirm what I already know—that he is dead. I have sat by this bedside for the past seven days since my father collapsed on his bedroom floor, brought down by a stroke that took his speech and doubled up his body and turned his eyes wild with alarm and set his hands shaking and grasping at things. The nurses know only his remains—that he has no pulse, that respiration has stopped, that his temperature has plunged, that his hair will continue to grow for some hours yet. They do not know that in my father's last moments the gift of his own father returned to his hands. They do not know that he took up the reins once more and, looking beyond his fear, drove himself into the sea.

This body of mine—eyes, ears, nose, lips, chin, forehead, height, weight—owes more to my father than to any other source. I look like him. Now, in these paragraphs, I discover that I think like him as well. I herein own him once and for all, the last of our differences resolved, the last of whatever opposition stood between our two natures put aside. I am my father's son. I carry the taste of him on my tongue. I hear in all I say the sound of his long silence. He survives in all I do and all I am. I have entered the deep waters with him.

GATHERING

*"All pure juxtaposition
is a gathering."*

THINGS

*The way in which you are
and I am, the manner in which
we humans are on earth . . . is dwelling.
To be a human being . . . means to dwell.*
—Martin Heidegger,
Building, Dwelling, Thinking

A January night. I wrap up in a scarf and push my hands into my pockets for the walk home from an evening lecture at the university. Cold moonlight silhouettes the winter-bared limbs that arch overhead: silver maples, twenty-one of them in all. Here, where I turn off Laburnum onto Sacramento Avenue, I can see most of these maples at a single glance. Just saplings when the city first set them out a half century ago, they line the avenue with trunks grown massive, their roots lifting the sidewalks, their limbs crossing each other from opposite curbs. I can count them: thirteen on the south side of the avenue, eight on the north. I can count as well the ones that will soon be missing—eleven of the largest maples condemned by the city as unsafe. They are slated to be cut down, three now, the others within the next two years. Tonight, for all their present beauty, the stark and shifting geometry of their shadowed limbs in patterns against the lighter sky, I cannot help but count the impending loss.

In midblock, a short strip of plastic ribbon tacked to a trunk marks the first of the trees to go. In the dark, I can't make out the color of the plastic but I know it to be orange. The ribbon flutters limply in the night breeze. Overhead, clouds drift southward. From the windows of the houses, patches of light fall onto the lawns. The ribbon-marked tree is a giant. Two large people could not join hands around its trunk. I know this, but something urges me to try. I push myself against the trunk, stretch my arms around the curve of its circumference, the side of my face flattened against the rough bark. I visualize my arms encircling the tree. I strain to bring the tips of my fingers together. Of course it's useless. I need help to do this. I let go.

Those of us who live on the two blocks of Sacramento Avenue between Laburnum and Palm have grown accustomed to the presence of these trees. Many of us have known them only in their maturity; nevertheless a few were here to see them planted, so that season by season, with quiet stealth, the trees came to overshadow the whole of their lives. Hardly any of them noticed this. These old-timers, after all, were intent on how their own children grew and how their grandchildren grew. All the while, the trees, in increments of hours, minutes, seconds, have stretched their limbs in ever widening arcs that tower now above the streets and rooftops, shading lawns where great-grandchildren take their first steps. Still, there were other matters to attend to. The trees grew out of mind, as it were.

But out of mind or not, the trees have filtered into the

lives of all of us who reside on the avenue. We wear the trees in our consciousness in the same unacknowledged way we wear our own skin or hear the sounds of our own voices. It is an intimacy that is likely to go unremarked. But when recent notice came from the city of the trees' impending removal, all of us on Sacramento Avenue realized at once the extent of their presence in our lives. "Why?" we asked. "Because they're old and ready to fall," we were told. Of course! We should have known: three widows on the block and another soon to be, her husband confined to a wheelchair, unable to breathe on his own. Still, it had not occurred to us that this selfsame mortality that overtakes our lives had overtaken the lives of the trees as well. We weren't any of us ready for it. We looked in dismay at those that were condemned, eleven of them, marked with splashes of paint, orange ribbons tacked to their trunks. We didn't see how we could give them up.

There's more to the narrative: episodes of political resistance, calls made to city officers; neighbors speaking out in opposition at council hearings; a tree-by-tree assessment led by the city forester, the rest of us tagging along to be shown the deterioration that requires each condemned tree to be cut; an offer from the city to get a second opinion by an independent arborist which, though granted, held out little hope that any of the trees would be spared; the final meeting with the city forester, all of us gathered by the forester's pickup on a late afternoon, the doomed trees with their orange ribbons visible up and down the block, the forester telling us that the second opinion concurred with the first.

The meeting dragged on; we were reluctant to break it off because we knew that when we did the whole thing was done, and the first of the trees could come down the very next day. Finally one of the neighbors spoke for us all when she asked, "Could you tell us when you're going to do it? I don't want to be home."

We're waiting now. Sometimes it's a little like holding one's breath. Something inheres in a thing like a tree or a park bench or a lamp by the bedside or the feel of one's own hand in a pocket or a stone found by the creek, something that so compels us, that so draws us within its sphere of influence that we feel shaped by its presence. It is this shaping presence that we stand to lose in the death of the Sacramento Avenue trees. It is a loss that reaches us beyond the mere loss of their familiarity, beyond the loss of whatever comfort of shade or enclosure they might provide, beyond even the loss of their beauty or the sheer length of their proximity to our lives. Beyond these moves a force arising from the pure juxtaposition of things, a force that draws us into being, that allows us to dwell fully in our lives.

All pure juxtaposition is a gathering. It gathers the Sacramento Avenue trees and those of us who live here into mutual dwelling, and through the agency of this dwelling, it gathers us into dwelling with all things. It roots us to the subsoil, raises our eyes to the sky, lifts us to the moon on night branches, speaks to us in veined leaf the language of the sun. It teaches us the dropping away that sheds itself, the moldering silence of deepest shade, the coming again in proper time. The naked power of juxtaposition to gather us into dwelling functions beyond any sentiment or thought of relationship. It is as direct and out of mind as our mutual exchange of carbon dioxide and oxygen. The trees literally breathe us and we them.

In the third stanza of his poem, "Melancholy Inside Families," Pablo Neruda pictures

> . . . a dining room where roses arrive,
> a dining room deserted
> as a fish bone. I am speaking of
> a smashed cup, a curtain, at the end
> of a deserted room. . . .

Here is a family sad with the failure to dwell. Neruda does not tell us what has precipitated this failure, but we are told that though the roses arrive, the room remains deserted, a dining room where dining fails. The room lacks the things needed to effect the gathering for which it is intended. What little it has—a smashed cup, a curtain—are not enough to gather the family into being. In this lack the family knows only the room's desertion, which the family receives as the emptiness we call melancholy.

To be otherwise the room would need the things of dining. It would need a table, for example, and utensils, plates, cups that are not smashed. It would need hunger and intent to dine. Only then could the deserted room enact its proper dwelling, gathering to it household and farm, the synthesis of sunlight and leaf, the thirst of roots for water. The measure of the authenticity of dwelling lies in this extension into relationship, drawing into mutuality not only the candle burning beside the roses, the folded napkin at plateside, the hushed recitation of gratitude, but plow and wheel as well, the bend of labor, weeding, sorting, harvesting, laying the pavement and rails of transport, extracting by pick and auger and shovel from beneath our very feet the metals with which we cook and eat. In our dining rooms we gather not only matters of manner and decorum, we gather the sweat of lives expended in darkness; we gather seasons and the passage of our planet round its native star.

Yet is not dwelling itself the invention of our thought of it? It is not that thought does not inhere in dwelling, it is that thought neither originates nor confirms it. The dwelling of which I speak is the sheer juxtaposition of things. It is not a gathering derivative of thought. Dwelling itself originates dwelling. Dwelling alone confirms dwelling.

So it is that we dwell in things with a surety beyond conscious perception. However set apart we might feel, there exists a concreteness in things that impinges directly and immediately upon our bodies, often sustaining connections we believe have been forfeited to circumstance.

In November of 1992, a year before my father died, I traveled to Orange County in southern California to visit my mother and him. My father, in his nineties, was seriously ill. Having barely survived a bout with pneumonia, his heart weakened, his body host to inoperable cancer, he spent most of his time in bed.

The house had two bedrooms, and in all my visits throughout the years, I had always slept in the spare bedroom. But on this visit, Mother brought me some bedding and showed me how to turn down a sleeping couch I didn't even know they owned. When I inquired about the spare bedroom, she told me she was sleeping there herself, that she had moved into it nearly three months before. The fact of this disclosure struck me with such a sense of strangeness, of disorder, that it must have shown in my face. My mother, speaking as if comforting a child, explained that she could not sleep with my father anymore; she would awaken in the night, unable to hear whether he was breathing or not. She would lie in the dark, straining to hear his breath, wondering if he had died. She had to move out, she explained. She couldn't take it anymore.

I didn't sleep that night. Sixty-five years earlier, my mother, not yet eighteen, my father, twenty-seven, had married. All those years they had bedded side by side. Now my father lay dying alone. My mother, like a transient guest, lay in the spare bedroom waiting out the certainty of what was to come.

In the morning while father was up, I went into his bedroom and shut the door behind me. I wanted to see for myself the scene of his solitary hours. What I found was that Mother's side of the bed, the whole side of the room that she had occupied, was perfectly preserved in every detail, like a memorial to her absence. She had taken nothing of herself to the spare bedroom. It was as if she had not left at all. At the dressing table lay her hair brush, comb, hand mirror, cosmetics, a silver box holding a few items of jewelry. My father had turned down the bedspread, Mother's pillow fluffed alongside his own as if she were coming to bed at any moment.

Among other items on the bedside table was a book of Mother's with a library marker inserted as though she had just put aside her reading. I took it up for a moment. I can't recall the title but whatever its content, the book told the truth: my father was not alone; Mother lay at his side as she always had. I put the book back on the table, careful to leave it as I had found it.

Count them. Eleven of the Sacramento Avenue maples will soon be cut down. Most of us have never known the avenue without them. Their loss will leave gaps in the arrangement of our lives. We have dwelt with these trees in ways deeper than thought can fathom. We have been gathered into being with them by force of simple presence. It is certain that when they are gone, we will be other than we are now. We will bear the shape of their absence.

THE CATCHING
CRATE

The catching crate was a structure designed by necessity and arrived at by means of error. It took its eventual form from what was left after the mistakes were discarded. What the crate was intended to catch was turkeys. My father raised turkeys for a living. Several times a year, each of the hundred thousand or so of these birds that were distributed over a 360-acre hillside of weeds and dust had to be caught. They had to be gotten in hand somehow for purposes of vaccination, breeder selection, or transportation to market. The catching crate figured so importantly in this need that it is hard to imagine how we could have managed without it.

All of us—my father, my brother and I, the farm hands, even my mother and little sister—called this simple structure "the catching crate," a name so frankly descriptive of its function that it seems somehow an unlikely appellation to have hit upon. I have no idea how it became so designated, but whenever we referred to it (as in "I'd like you to set up the catching crate over by the breeder pens"), that was the term invariably applied. It was a name spoken in reverence and aversion.

Those of us who worked with it hated the catching

crate, but the alternatives—or rather the lack of them—were even more hateful. To catch turkeys in the thing was to know that misery is relative. We were always thankful that our situation wasn't worse. Since "worse" would have been more or less intolerable, we looked upon the catching crate as a sort of saving presence, and our loathing of the task associated with it was tempered with a grudging yet heartfelt gratitude verging on the religious. This needs explaining.

Turkeys are hard to catch. They're hard enough even to contain. Just to get them into some kind of enclosure and keep them there long enough to get your hands on them is an ambition fraught with serious difficulties. For one thing, turkeys can fly, not well, but well enough to get them sufficiently airborne to clear an eight-foot fence. So you can't just herd a bunch of turkeys into a corner, hoping to contain them while you catch them one at a time. As soon as you grab for the first one, the others, frantic to escape, explode upward in a colliding tangle of thrashing wings. They pile into a great heap against the fence, claws scratching for a foothold, straining to get to the top, some scrabbling over the fence and dropping off on the back side, a few managing to get airborne and, in a directionless frenzy of flight, crashing into the fence or each other or into whoever is trying to catch them. As comic as this may seem, the dark side is that the birds trapped on the bottom of the heap are being smothered to death, their bodies raked by the claws of those above them.

When you realize what is happening and start throwing turkeys off the top trying to save those underneath, you find yourself reaching down into a pile of limp turkey carcasses, their feathers wet with smeared manure and blood. When my father first went into the turkey business, we tried to catch turkeys this way. We ran a bunch of them into a corner and started grabbing. It was a method abandoned on first try.

A second difficulty in catching turkeys is that they're big. A full-grown tom weighs as much as forty pounds, a hen, thirty. In turkeys bred for the table, a lot of that weight is concentrated in the breast muscle, and it is this powerful muscle that drives the wings and legs. This accounts for the third major difficulty, which is that turkeys are strong. So even if by chance and adjustment you eventually design a catching crate that is portable, strong, yet light enough to be moved, a crate that restricts the birds' flight and prevents their piling up, you will still find that the twenty-five to fifty birds you hope to contain in the crate will simply walk away with it unless it is staked to the ground. Attaching it to a floor, we discovered, proved useless. The turkeys clawed it out of the floor in a matter of hours.

The aesthetics of beauty has always recognized simplicity of form as a fundamental artistic virtue. This is not to say that we should admire any object that happens to lack in complexity; such a thing might be merely dull. The simplicity I speak of has an inevitability about it that suggests that a form cannot be otherwise than exactly as it is. It is frequently a form required by utility. The lines of a canoe or sailing ship, for example, bear a clean and unadorned beauty necessitated by function. The catching crate was like this. It could be nothing other than what it was.

After all the modified fence corners, the cages of various designs, the darkened and lidded boxes, the adjustable squeeze chutes that could never be made to accommodate more than a dozen turkeys, the structure that finally emerged was a simple three-sided containment that could hold up to three dozen turkeys at a time. It consisted of two right-triangle side pieces fronted by a gate, which could be shut after the turkeys were driven inside. The back of the crate—and here is where the genius of its design was realized—was a panel angled at forty-five degrees. The crate was built of slats, because we had discovered that although turkeys balked at entering a solid structure, they walked unperturbed into one they could see through. They would try to push right on out the back, thus wedging themselves into the slant. This prevented them from piling up and being injured. With the gate closed, there was just enough room for a single man, kneeling on pads, to reach in and grab the turkeys by their legs.

The catching crate was a thing of spare beauty for which none of us could fully suppress our admiration. We manifested in its presence a sort of vaguely felt humility, an attitude of deference that fell just short of piety.

The catching itself had strong elements of ritual. For one thing, it had to be done kneeling. For another, it exacted of the catcher a discipline of some severity in order to stay at the task more than a few minutes. In other words, catching turkeys required character. To catch a turkey, you must put on a pair of stout leather gloves, get down on your knees in the opening of the catching crate, pick out a pair of legs that belong to a single turkey, and make a swift, hard, backhanded stab at them, hoping to pin the legs together in your grip so that you can yank the bird off its feet before it loosens one of its legs and claws itself free of you.

A frightened turkey always shits. I do not use that term if it can be avoided, preferring *defecate* for the verb and *manure* or *feces* for the noun. But none of these is adequate for what a turkey does. Fresh turkey manure is a smeary mess of yellows, greens, and whites that smells utterly vile and has the unfortunate consistency of soft pudding. When the catcher yanks the turkey's feet out from under it, those feet are standing in a pile of this stuff. It flicks back on the catcher, again and again, until the catcher is plastered with it from where his knees contact the ground right up to his throat and, not infrequently, even into his face and hair. As the hours go on and load after load of turkeys is herded into it, the conditions in the crate grow worse. The front of the catcher's clothes stiffen on him with accumulating layers of turkey shit. To do his job, the catcher has to endure the inevitable humiliation of spitting and wiping shit from his eyes while everyone else can see what happens. No one ever offers help. No one ever laughs. Will I be thought absurdly romantic if I insist that the ritual of catching asked of us who did it a common trust that was truly sacred?

Yet there was a time when we almost lost faith, a dangerous time, a crisis, that happened to coincide with my own childhood initiation into catching. I was eleven years old. At that age, I was already used to long hours of work because my father, believing that work alone was the salvation of manhood and that training in it couldn't begin too soon, had put me seriously to work when I was barely eight. Any time I wasn't in school, I was at work. My eleventh year was also the year when Hector Berrens, driving home from the farm with the sun in his eyes, crashed into the rear end of a parked truck.

There were five hired hands on the farm who, along with my father and my brother, Rowland, and I, could make up a crew of eight for any major handling of the birds. The hired hands had been taken on over the years as the flock grew. Al Messeral had been the first, hired when I was just a baby. Pete Haney came next, a refugee from Depression-era Oklahoma; then Bob Townsley, who had lost his sharecropping rights to a small plot of gravelly ground in southern Arkansas. Hector and his brother, Ernie, arrived only a year before the accident.

Hector had come asking for work when the eighty-acre lease he horse-farmed was sold and he was left with no means to provide for his aging parents and for Ernie, who was retarded and could not make it on his own. Hector had never married. He had been unwaveringly obedient to his father's request that he "stay home and take care of things." I would have to judge that, in any intellectual or reflective way, Hector was not very bright. Yet he carried himself with a degree of dignity that even a child such as I could sense. He came to my father's office, standing dark and stocky in the doorway, a powerful man, big boned, with a thick neck and broad forehead, and hat in hand, he requested work. He offered Ernie at half wages, saying that Ernie was a hard worker but that they would have to work together since no one else could understand him. Father, realizing he needed more help, took the two of them on.

The next morning Hector was there at dawn, wearing new work gloves and carrying a lunch pail. As he came to where we had gathered by the feed barn, his face bore a certain characteristic flatness of expression that suggested reserve or resignation perhaps, or maybe just dullness. Ernie trotted alongside him in little spurts and stalls like a squirrel that can't quite make up its mind whether or not to finish crossing the road. He clutched his lunch pail in both hands as if he thought someone might take it from him, and his eyes, a little wild, darted from face to face. Hector had to calm him, show him where to stand, and separate him from his lunch pail so that their lunches could be put up in the lunch room. It was later that same day that a danger, grave with consequence for us all, first arose.

We were in the midst of breeder selection, a process requiring us to go through the whole flock of a hundred thousand turkeys, separating the breeders from the market birds. This meant that in the space of a few weeks every turkey on the farm would have to be caught. The catching had always been shared. Al might catch for an hour or so, then Pete and Bob, then Al again. Taking turns was the way it had always been done, invariable in the years since I had been put to work on these crews. Except for an occasional grab at a turkey or two, I had not yet taken my first turn in the catching crate.

I'm not a big man now, and then, only ten years old, I was small for my age and thin. It was all I could manage to hoist a full-grown turkey onto a bench top for vaccination or wing banding. It was understood that catching was still beyond my strength and beyond that of Rowland, two years older than me, as well. I never saw Father catch. It seemed obvious to me that he had more important jobs to do.

On that first day of Hector's and Ernie's employment, there were eight of us hanging birds on a scale in front of Father, who sat on a stool checking their weight and feeling them to see which would make the best breeders. Al, Pete, and Bob took turns catching. If a bird was going to market, we released it into the field; if it was a breeder, we dragged it along a bench top to be banded and dusted for mites. Then we dropped it into the breeder enclosure. Hour after hour we circled from scale to bench to catching crate, where the catcher—his knees in filth, splattered, scratched, stung by the incessant thrashing of stubby wing tips—hauled out turkeys for us.

About mid-morning, Hector, seeing how things were done, strapped on the knee pads and took a turn. He made the usual mistakes of a beginner: he grabbed only one leg and the turkey clawed itself loose with the free one; he failed to guard against the bird that had turned itself in the crate and, all forty pounds of it, launched itself from the back of his neck out the opening. He learned through sheer error how to look away at the right moment, his eye glasses, with their scratchy lenses taped onto the frame, so splattered that he had to wash them off at the turkey trough in order to see what he was doing. But by the time Hector finished his turn he was doing as well as anyone could expect.

As near as I can remember, it was a little before eleven when Al said to Hector, "If I can get you to give up those knee pads, I'll take over for a while." I heard Hector say something to the effect that he would take a turn for Ernie, since we could all see that Ernie was not up to the task. How this could have happened I don't know but, after the most mild protest, Al let him do it. We all let him do it. We let Hector go back down on his knees and catch the turkeys Ernie couldn't catch. As a child, I simply remember feeling that something was terribly wrong. I know now that we had put ourselves in jeopardy. We stood to lose what we might never be able to reclaim. When we shut down for lunch that day, Hector was still in the catching crate.

After that the situation worsened. Hector, first insisting on catching for Ernie, later resisted being relieved from the task at all. He would be the first one in the catching crate in the morning, and it was hard to get him out of there. He took on this hardest and dirtiest of our labors as his natural lot, putting his hands to the task as though, by right of some inherent virtue lacking in himself, the rest of us deserved better. He deferred to us in everything, anxious to sacrifice himself to us as he had to his father. In the beginning the others tried to take their turns, but when he declined, they were willing to let him have his way. By the second year of Hector's employment, no one even made a pretense anymore. Hector did all the catching.

We had lost our way. Even I knew this. We had forfeited the one ceremony that, above all others, redeemed the misery of our work. We had forgotten the forms and words—"Here, let me spell you for a bit"—of a liturgy that had once bound us together in common regard. In the off season we would come upon the catching crate idle in some corner of a field, weeds sprouting up through the slats. None of us could look at it without knowing our loss.

Hector saw the truck at the last second, too late to avoid hitting it but not too late to jam on the brakes. Ernie was thrown under the dash, which probably saved his life. Hector, with his great power, had kept his grip on the steering wheel, the impact bending it over against the dash. Hector managed to stay in the car, his head slamming into the liner above the windshield. In less than a week he was back at work, his head stitched and wrapped in bandages that made his hat perch off to one side, an angry swelling above one eye. His eyeglasses had somehow survived, though they were patched up even more than before. We were in the midst of breeder selection again and everyone watched Hector put on the knee pads, drop to his knees in the catching crate, and begin catching. Father, sitting on his stool, watched him, Al and Pete and Bob watched him; Rowland and I watched him.

Before an hour had gone by, Al put on the pads and began catching, quietly insisting to Hector that that was the way it was going to be. Seeing this, I resolved that when Al was done I would take a turn. When I asked Al for the pads, he at first looked questioningly at me, then handed them over.

The turkeys were hard for me to hang onto and to drag out the opening. It didn't matter how hard it was. Al had taken his turn and now I was taking mine. Afterwards, Pete would take his, and then Bob, and maybe even Rowland. We had found our refuge again. There, under the slanting roof of the catching crate with its two triangular sides and a gate that snapped in place, I knelt, as in prayer, paying homage to the site of our return.

GATHERING

The gravestone is inscribed "Ritchie W. Evans, 1936–1994." It is only one of the dozens of grave-markers that I pass on my morning walk through the old cemetery at the end of Washington Avenue in Chico, California. Beyond this scant information, I know nothing whatsoever about Ritchie Evans. What with all of the more elaborate gravemarkers in the cemetery, some with beauti-fully artistic sculptures, I might never have noticed Ritchie's modest grave had it not been for the fresh flowers that were so persistently placed there.

This regular exchange of new flowers for old had been going on for some time, I believe, before I actually regis-tered the fact. But once I noticed, I saw that the procedure was absolutely punctual. Even in the darkest weeks of win-ter, even when one of the severest wind storms of the decade toppled trees all over town, Ritchie's grave received fresh flowers.

And then one morning in early February, I saw who it was that tended Ritchie's grave. She was wearing a pale yellow dress with a shawl pulled over her shoulders and a scarf over her hair, and she was arranging some flowers in the little plastic cone that is standard on all the newer graves in the cemetery. It had rained heavily during the night, and a light mist dropped onto the cemetery grounds and drifted down on her where she kneeled by Ritchie's grave. She looked up as I approached, and our eyes met. I said, "You keep the grave looking nice." She looked at her hands, idly rearranged a few flowers, glanced back at me, and said, "It seems the least I can do." That was all that passed between us. She turned back to her flowers, and I went on with my walk.

I have not seen her since, but my thoughts often return with her to tend Ritchie's grave. Something of her act and her will bends me to this task. I bear flowers with her into all my days, and everywhere the sharp odor of cut stems accompanies me. The simple logic of her few words ("the least I can do") rises unspoken into the pauses of my most ordinary conversation. I awaken sometimes in the early light of my own bedroom to find that my mind has settled on her like dew settling on the cemetery lawns. What is it that impels me toward so common a thing? What do I owe Ritchie Evans or the woman who tends his grave? What do I owe any of those souls whose faceless graves accompany my morning walks?

Not long after I had chanced upon the woman, I met up

with two young workers seeding lawn at the cemetery. I commented that with summer heat coming on I thought they had a pleasant job working there under the canopy of oaks and maples with sprinklers going all around them. One of the two smoothed the ground adjacent to a family burial site, pulling a rake through the freshly dug soil. "I work around names of people like this every day," he said, gesturing toward one of the family gravestones with the head of his rake. "It makes me want to take care of my life. I mean there are things I don't want to waste myself on." He kept on raking, and his eyes followed his own movements as he talked. "When I go home from work and my wife is cooking or something, and she's only twenty-six years old, and I know she'll be nothing but a name like this some day. This job is good for knowing stuff like that."

Along with his gloves and his lunch pail, this young husband took what he now knew home with him each day from work. He carried it into his very household where it fell like sorrow upon the limbs and eyes of his wife as she set out their supper. Even in the sanctuary of his home, perhaps especially there, he read in the lettering inscribed on every gravestone in the cemetery the spelling of his own name as well. For whatever reason, he wanted me to know this. He did not tell me in great regret or dread, but in some newly dug warmth of heart. He was learning how our mortality runs deeply into our affections, how our capacity to love resides within our capacity to die.

A few months after these encounters at the cemetery, the Olympic flame made a stopover in Chico on its way to the summer games. Lots of events were planned for the occasion, including some evening music at the Children's Park. So after supper my wife, Karen, and I walked uptown to join in the celebration. Karen had heard that a replica of the Vietnam Veterans' Memorial was to be displayed on the south lawn of Chico State University's Kendall Hall. She thought she would like to see this memorial, and we decided to do so on our way to the Children's Park.

The memorial consisted of 128 sectioned panels made of some hard material resembling the dark granite of the Washington original. The panels were four feet high and joined end to end so that they formed two long walls that converged at an angle in the exact center of the display. The angle of the panels was such that, when Karen and I stood at the center of the wall, the far ends of it curved around us on both sides. From there, we could see all the names, 58,494 of them, etched in silver and stretching for 250 feet across the south lawn of Kendall Hall. I put a hand to the wall, feeling the lettering there, touching the last remnants of lives just like my own. And others did the same: a young student, who had come seeking the name of a friend, touched each letter of his name as tenderly as though they were her own eyelids; an older couple lifted a child up to pet a name as if it were a puppy; a bearded man with a knapsack over his shoulder pressed his forehead to the wall, and his lips silently recited something that needed to be said.

In the hollow beyond the display, I could see the university rose garden illuminated in the evening light. Close by, the waters of Chico Creek ran through deepening shadows toward the sea. From the Children's Park, I could hear the sound of instruments and singing and the excited voices of children playing. It seemed for the moment that my townspeople and I were gathering at the absolute junction where the circle closes, where all our going travels in one direction, where a soldier's last cry can be heard in a child's laughter and love blooms in every occasion.

In the Children's Park, the gospel choir was singing. I stood on the lawn in front of the bandstand and the voices of the singers resonated through me. Children ran about the grounds, their calls shrill with excitement. The crowd clapped their hands in rhythm to the singing, and the choir clapped, and a young woman in a wheelchair next to me clapped. The woman in the wheelchair was impaired by some disease so that her arms flailed wildly in spasmodic jerks, and her hands frequently failed to strike each other, crossing crazily in midair. She clapped in pure abandonment, her face twisting up in distorted smiles of joy. A short distance away, Karen sat on a bench under a tree. In the cemetery beyond the avenues, Ritchie Evans lay in his grave.

I am not the woman in the wheelchair whose joy shakes through me like some spasm of my own. I am not the singers on the bandstand whose song forms itself in my own throat. I am not Karen watching from a bench under the limbs of a tree in whose shelter I rest as well. I am not the children playing nor am I any one of the 58,494 lives whose end is recorded on the south lawn of Kendall Hall. I am not Ritchie Evans nor the woman who tends his grave nor the chastened husband whose work in the Chico cemetery teaches him daily that his young wife must someday die.

I am not the one who has known and now tells of these things, for I am ever and inseparably receiving myself from within the lives of all these others. I draw my very being from this common existence, as wholly and finally and inextricably and repeatedly as breath itself is drawn from undivided air.

What I owe Ritchie Evans is what I owe myself. What any of us owes him is exactly that. Ritchie lies within the gravesite of our collective being. He persists within the common journey of our species from 1936 to 1994. All his doings are as our own. To keep him in mind is to keep ourselves in mind. We are all of us tending the dead, and the dead tend us as well.

I do not have to know anything particular about Ritchie Evans to know I bear his life within my own and that I would do so had he lived his fifty-eight years somewhere on the far side of the planet in some ancient culture lost now to memory. The woman in the yellow dress tends Ritchie's grave for us all. Week after week her remembering hands lay flowers at the very feet of our passing here. The flowers are fragrant and newly cut. We bend with her now to lay them, stem and leaf and blossom, at the exact site of all our going on.

Occasionally on my morning walk, I discover Ritchie's flowers blown over by some night wind. I can't pass by without straightening them up. It seems the least I can do.

"We need to know that joy itself holds conversation in the dark."

THE DEBEAKING
MACHINE

Ernie was the only one who openly dissented. The rest of us insisted that the process was painless. We did so, reciting this fiction chapter and verse with the anxious certainty of believers whose faith is called to question by fact. We had to believe it didn't hurt.

Ernie's lone dissent could easily be discounted because he was only Hector's retarded brother. He couldn't read. He couldn't write. He couldn't even carry on a conversation that anyone other than Hector could understand. Hector had to supervise everything Ernie did. So what could Ernie possibly know about how much pain a turkey might or might not feel? Besides, Father said it didn't hurt, that it was no different than trimming a toenail as long as you were careful not to cut "into the quick." I was only twelve at the advent of the debeaking machine, and I clung unwaveringly to Father's reassurance. I didn't want to admit to yet another shame among the shameful acts I already felt myself involved in.

The debeaking machine was delivered to the farm by the company representative himself, and he demonstrated its use on the morning of the very day we debeaked our first flock of five thousand turkeys. The company brochure that Father had studied for some weeks prior to ordering the machine advised that it was best to debeak turkeys while they were still young to minimize any shock the birds might feel from the procedure. "The older the turkey, the greater the stress," the pamphlet explained. It was an item of advice similar to that given to mothers to have their infant sons circumcised while they are still young enough that it doesn't hurt, a theory flatly contradicted by the response of any baby whose foreskin is being cut away.

Nonetheless, our first "debeakers" were little more than a month old. They hadn't acquired their true feathers yet and were still caged in the rows of coops they occupied before being put out on the range. On the morning of the demonstration, Al Messeral, the farm foreman, Bob Townsley, Hector and Ernie Berrens, and I were all waiting at 7:00 A.M. when the company representative drove up. Father came out from the house, and the two of them got the machine out of the trunk of the representative's car. Al had already strung an extension cord from the barn to the coops, so everything was set for the demonstration to take place.

The representative, who introduced himself as Terence Ferguson ("Just call me Fergy"), was dressed in a dark suit with a white shirt and tie. Even with a shop apron strapped on to protect his clothing, he looked impossibly out of place standing among the rest of us with the smell of manure rising and the hum of flies all about. He began his instruction by emphasizing what we already knew: that some form of debeaking was essential to prevent cannibalism. He stressed the word *essential* as if to imply that it might be a debatable point. But of course he was right.

Even with a hundred acres of fenced range to accommodate the hundred thousand turkeys my father raised annually, that's still a thousand birds an acre, a density intolerable for turkeys, whose nature it is to gather secretively in small family flocks. They are animals wholly unprepared to deal with crowding, and their response to the distress this raises is to eat each other. They pick and stab with their sharp beaks until blood is drawn. Then they converge on the bloodied one, standing and pecking at it or taking swipes at it in passing. The victim, still on its feet, wanders about the flock with bloody, gaping holes in its body and half its head pecked away. Some seem unable to fall and die. By the time of the debeaking machine, I had seen one such bloodied horror sitting at roost with both its eyes eaten away, acting on one of its few surviving instincts, asleep side by side with the others, as though being eaten alive were the natural order of things.

All of us who lived or worked on the farm suffered with the knowledge of this hideous aberration. We didn't like to think that such a thing was of our own doing, though we knew it was. Even as a child of twelve I felt the taint of this as a shameful wrong in which we all somehow partook. Father invariably reduced the whole matter to terms of economic loss, complaining that he couldn't afford to lose so many mature birds, that the cost of it would drive him out of business. In the very vigor of his protest, he disclosed the presence of an uneasy conscience. We all had more than enough cause to want to believe in the efficacy and humaneness of the debeaking machine.

We stood around Terence Ferguson that morning eyeing him, in his black suit and tie, with wariness and hope, while he pointed out to us, with a fair degree of proprietary pride, the various patented components of the debeaking machine. It was an almost preposterously simple mechanism for something so expensive. The whole thing consisted of little more than a stationary metal bite rod, about the thickness of a pencil, with a movable, electrically heated, red-hot blade positioned above it. The idea was to split the turkey's bill over the bite rod with the upper half exposed on top so that the electrified blade could sear it off. A foot pedal operated the blade, which sprung back up when the pedal was released. These working parts were mounted in the open end of a sort of hinged box set on three legs adjustable for height like those of a tripod.

By the time Ferguson had finished with these funda-mentals, two other farm hands, Pete Haney and Jim Bunton, and my fourteen-year-old brother, Rowland, had joined the six of us who were already there. Father had called them in from their work because he wanted every-one to be properly instructed in the use of the machine. Ferguson, who seemed to relish this increase in his audi-ence, recounted a few particulars the others had missed. Rubbing his hands together as if in anticipation of doing something quite extraordinary, he said, "Well, then, let's get started, shall we?"

Hector grabbed a turkey out of the coop and handed it to Ferguson. It was a scruffy looking thing, half fuzz and half real feathers. A turkey that age has lost all the plump, downy appearance of a hatchling and has become little more than a pair of twiggy legs supporting a sort of prickly, half-naked body with a few wing feathers and a knot of fuzz, like a boy's flat-top, sticking up on the crown of its head. If you look at its face straight on, a bird like this appears crazed. Ferguson took the turkey from Hector, letting it hang from the tips of his fingers by legs that looked about as sturdy as strips of dry spaghetti. He held it up to the debeaking machine, the ball of his foot cocked above the pedal in readiness to push down. The rest of us crowded in around him. Ferguson, absorbed in the particulars of his demonstration, explained that the prescribed procedure for a right-handed operator was to "hold the bird's legs with your left hand while forcing its bill apart with the forefinger of your right hand." We weren't hearing much of what he said because we could all see the electrically heated blade, glowing red in the open face of the machine.

Ferguson had trouble getting the demonstration turkey's bill pried open. I could see that this flustered him considerably. When he finally managed to get the job done and had the head of the bird shoved into the debeaker with its bill split over the bite bar, he paused to give final instructions on the depth of cut, which, he explained, was crucial to the operation. "If you don't cut off enough," he said, "it'll grow back before you market the bird and you still have to contend with cannibalism. It's like getting your money's worth out of a haircut. You need to whack off enough so that it lasts awhile." With that, he was ready to make the cut. I actually saw his foot start to compress the pedal, but before he could continue, I heard myself asking with more urgency than I intended, "Does it hurt?"

"Does it hurt to cut your toenail?" he responded. He sounded annoyed. "Just don't cut into the quick." At the time, I didn't know what the quick was, but before I could follow up on this, Ferguson pressed down on the pedal, and we could all see for ourselves that debeaking a turkey was nothing like cutting a toenail. And I suppose it was exactly then, when we saw how dreadful it really was, that we became such religious adherents of Ferguson's toenail theory, silencing thereafter any suggestion to the contrary with our own glib reassurances.

I expected to see just the tip of the beak cut away, but Ferguson made the cut so deep that the bird was left with nothing more than a charred stump barely long enough to accommodate its nostrils. The blade burned its way through with intolerable slowness. You could hear it sizzle. A kind of oily smoke curled up around Ferguson, making him look all the more remarkable in his suit and tie. When he pulled the turkey's head out of the machine to check the cut, blood was oozing from it. So he shoved it back in and sort of smeared the stump back and forth against the hot blade for a few seconds, explaining that it was important to "seal the cut" adequately. I don't know what it looked like to Ferguson, but to the rest of us the face of that little bird looked something like a cigarette butt that had burned itself out. He handed it to Hector, and Hector dumped it back in the coop where it stood teetering for a moment before its legs folded under it and it came to rest on the wire in a sort of shocked daze.

Ferguson demonstrated a few more times, and then each of us had to take a turn. We all tried to get away with a cut shallower than was prescribed, but Ferguson would have no part of such squeamishness. And neither would Father, who pinned his hopes on the machine's efficacy to save him from heavy losses. Al went first, and then Hector, Bob, Jim, Rowland, Father, and me, in that order. Ernie refused his turn, and Hector said that it was okay, he didn't have to do it. By the second go-round, we had all learned to keep our fingers as far from the hot blade as possible and to lean away from the rising smoke because the smell was so bad. Before the hour was out, Ferguson, satisfied with our progress, had stripped off his shop apron and was gone. Father was back in the farm office, the others had returned to their earlier work, and the four of us who made up the day's crew were left with five thousand turkeys to debeak by nightfall.

At noon Ernie wouldn't eat his lunch. He sat beside Hector with his lunch pail on his lap, but he wouldn't open it. At length Hector opened it for him and showed him that the sandwiches were the same as his own and that they were good and he should eat them. "Cold ham, Ernie. You like cold ham." But Ernie was indifferent to these appeals, seeming not to hear them at all, the open lunch pail resting across his knees with his ham sandwich still wrapped in wax paper, an apple and a thermos of coffee untouched.

He'd been like this all morning. We'd divided up the work so that Hector and I took turns catching and debeaking, Al administered vaccinations, and Ernie returned the turkeys to the coop. Hector, who took the first turn catching, leaned into the coop and brought out a turkey that I debeaked. The plan was that Ernie would take the turkey from me, pass it to Al to be vaccinated and release it into the coop. But when I pulled the debeaked turkey off the blade and tried to hand it to him, Ernie wouldn't take it from me. I held it out to him, but he shook his head and backed away, leaving the bird dangling from my fingers. Hector finally got him to take the it. Things went fairly smoothly for a while, but then Ernie suddenly balked again. This went on throughout the morning, and once he even walked away from the job. When Hector brought him back, Ernie kept repeating, "It's no good, Hector. It's no good. No good. No good."

Of course it was no good. We all knew it was no good, which is precisely why we had to concur when Al parroted Ferguson and said, "It doesn't hurt them, Ernie; it's just like cutting your toenails." But Ernie wasn't capable of maintaining this painfully obvious lie we'd chosen to tell ourselves. His innocence exposed us and made our own dishonesty nearly intolerable.

The morning after that first day of debeaking, I woke up early and troubled. The farm was silent, the turkeys still at roost, the bedroom windows without light. I thought of the rows of coops lined up in the dark beyond the barn. They would be wet now with fog drawn off the sea, the corrugated metal roofs beaded with drops of water, the wire floors cold to the touch. I wondered how a baby turkey could eat with half its bill gone. Some of the turkeys had literally gasped when I pulled them back off the blade, as if they'd been holding their breath, as if I'd punched the air out of them. I looked up into the dark, Rowland asleep beside me in the bed we shared. I wanted to wake him up.

Instead I slipped out of bed and, pulling on my clothes, went out.

The turkeys were just beginning to stir when I got to the coops. Turkeys don't sleep in; the whole flock gets up at once. I had witnessed it hundreds of times, but I had never seen a flock awaken to anything quite like the conditions of that morning. They appeared bewildered by what had happened to them. Some looked as if they hadn't gone to roost at all but had spent the night on their feet, their eyes a lusterless vacancy, their heads hanging down. Others tried to eat, stabbing repeatedly at the mash and pellets in the feed trays, uncomprehending as to why they couldn't eat. Though Hector and I had cauterized the wounds until we feared the heat itself would kill the birds, most that morning dripped blood from the stumps of their amputated beaks. Everything was smeared red: the feed, the trays, the frame and wire of the coops, the turkeys themselves. Blood dripped onto the ground below. The water in the crocks darkened. In every coop a few birds lay dead.

I gathered up the dead ones, counting them as I went, fifty-six in all, a loss that Father later that morning would favorably compare to the losses he hoped to avoid. I heaped up the feed trays in the hope that the birds might get more food in their mouths. I emptied the bloodied crocks and put in fresh water. And I would have done more could I have thought of anything more to do. I had need of more to do, for the sun, breaking over the eastern horizon, dissolved the obscuring fog and laid bare to hard sight the consequence of all our doings. It opened itself on my mind as surely and unequivocally as Ernie's proffered lunch had opened on his, demanding that I choose what I was willing to swallow. I stood by the little pile of dead turkeys gathered from the coops. They smelled like burnt garbage. Their silenced lives rose in my ears like the voice of deepest conscience, asking that I not turn away. "It's no good, Hector. It's no good, Al. It's no good, Linley." But I did turn away. All of us except Ernie, who wasn't clever enough to outwit himself, turned away.

Years beyond and hundreds of thousands of turkeys later, I would come to understand what a grave turning away it was. Meanwhile I would do what I was told. We had to put a stop to the cannibalism didn't we?

I washed and went to breakfast.

NIGHT TALK

Conversations
in Darkness

My wife, Karen, awakened me in the middle of the night a few weeks ago to tell me that she loves me. I lay looking up into the darkness while Karen, on her side facing me, explained as carefully and completely as she could exactly how much and why she loved me. She had thrown an arm over me, and as she talked, she patted me in a most comforting way and tucked the bedding around my shoulders to keep out the winter chill. She told me that I was the best thing that had ever happened to her and that no one had ever listened to her or cared about her in the way that I do. She thanked me for the most ordinary things: cooking supper, cleaning up around the house, changing the bedding, helping her to word a letter to the editor that she was particularly concerned to get right. She told me that I am her "very best friend" and how sad it is to think that some people never have a friend like that. She herself, she explained, might have gone her whole life without such a friend, might have died without having known anyone who truly loved her.

Then with the deepest seriousness she said, "Please be careful when you work on the roof tomorrow. I don't know what I'd do if something happened to you." I heard the urgency in her, the voice of that old, plaintive wish that what was certain to happen someday would please not happen yet. Her words, spoken in the dark of the night, came themselves from another darkness we each knew only too well. The fifteen years that separate our ages occupied the room like a third presence. It passed like a shadow across the east windows where the sycamore limbs swayed under the lash of a wind-driven rain; it sat on the foot of the bed, pressed the weight of itself upon our limbs and chests so that we had to labor to breathe, insinuated itself under the covers where it worked to wedge itself between us.

When Karen reaches my present age, I will be eighty—should I live that long. She is almost certain to end her life alone. How often since first we talked of this and chose nonetheless to join our lives together, has this outcome passed in detail before my eyes? I see the bag of groceries hauled home from the market, the key turned in the doorlock of a darkened house, lights switched on, a supper cooked and eaten alone. What does one do when the supper things are put away, shower taken, phone calls made, reading grown stale? Sometimes when I am absorbed in some task as I am now, writing these words, Karen's voice will reach me from another room: "Lin, come and talk with me awhile." I cannot bear the thought of that solitary call resonating, unheard, unanswered, through the vacant rooms.

Yet within these haunting fears lives a tenderness that lights my cheeks like the afterglow of a long day spent in the sun. My face, my eyes, throat, arms, hands, my speech and thoughts and feelings radiate, like the night stones of some south-facing wall, a warmth that darkness itself seems to generate. From the certain prospect of our untimely separation there arises between Karen and me a night talk of such unrestrained disclosure that nowhere else can we discover its like. It is the darkest and bravest of our conversations, requiring a language that gives all, says all, goes utterly unprotected. At such moments, our words clothe dread itself in garments of deliverance, and that which most threatens us most frees us and places our hearts unguarded into each other's hands.

When I was in my early twenties, I suffered such a painful falling out with my parents that the estrangement lasted for nearly three years. During that time the three of us spoke not one word to each other. I was accused of an act of which I was innocent and said so. My mother, swayed by circumstances that suggested otherwise, remained convinced of my guilt. As to the exact nature of the accusation, let me just say that it was sufficiently serious and was made, I believe, in error rather than malice. Still, Mother's certainty of my guilt brought not only my father but my brother and sister toward the same opinion as well. At the time, I was employed on the family farm and had every intention of making it my life's work. Instead, I left the farm within the hour of my being accused and never worked there again.

I found a job on a remote poultry farm twenty miles east of Palmdale in California's Mojave Desert. But the farm soon went bankrupt and I ended up working at a Chevron station on the outskirts of town. It was there on an August afternoon in 120-degree heat that had so softened the asphalt on the station's driveway that the soles of my shoes stuck to it, that Mother broke the long silence.

I was literally at the driver's side door, waiting for the window to be rolled down, before I realized who it was that had pulled up to the pump. Father was at the wheel. He glanced up at my face, startled to see me there. He looked away and then at Mother in the passenger seat. He was obviously unsettled and unsure as to what he should do. Mother said, "Well, hello there!" Her voice reached me, false with feigned casualness, from the far seat. I don't remember whether I hesitated, took a breath, swallowed, or what. All I remember is hearing myself ask, "Would you like regular or high octane?" Father answered, "High octane would be fine." I filled the tank, checked the oil and water, cleaned the windshield, took their money, and walked away.

I could barely breathe. I fled toward the rear of the station so as to avoid the others in the lube room. The rear of the station was treeless, the station wall baking in the heat. In the inch or two of shade afforded by a dumpster stacked with discarded tires, I stopped to catch my breath. And then Mother was there, her face flushed dangerously red with the heat, which she had never tolerated well. She came up to me where I stood backed against the dumpster. She said, "Linley, this has gone far enough." She tried to sound firm yet calm like a scolding mother who needs to correct the error of her child. But as she spoke the words, her false teeth (as dentures were more honestly called in those days) slipped a little, causing a clicking sound. Mother, who had always been terribly sensitive about this, brought her hand up to cover her mouth. She had no hat and so she squinted against the sun that poured down on us and reflected off the station wall. Sweat formed in the creases of her neck. Behind the screen of her hand, I could see her mouth work, as she tried to press her teeth back in place with her tongue. Finally, all her dignity undone, whatever small pride she had been able to retain compromised, she had to stick her fingers in her mouth to adjust her teeth. When she spoke again, her voice came unguarded, carrying the grief of her three years' sorrow: "Son, it's time we ended this."

Of course it was time. But I saw in her, in the tilt of her head perhaps, or something in her eyes, that her opinion of my guilt was unaltered. What she offered was a mother's forgiveness; she was willing to let the trespass go unadmitted and unanswered so that she could have her child once more. Her love required this, making its appeal from the pain of its own loss. I saw this, but the error of it all, the everlasting injustice of it, made her offer of forgiveness as deadly to me as a drink of poison. In the end, I could say nothing. She tried to hold my eyes, her own imploring me to let the hardness go, but when she saw that I couldn't or wouldn't, her chin quivered and she blinked and turned away.

Later, my eyes stung with a sudden rush of hot tears, I vomited all my bitterness into the station toilet. Kneeling on the floor of the stall, afraid that I would be found there, I touched within my mother's dark pain and my own a love for her more fierce and unchecked than any I had ever known.

Our deepest love dwells in the house of woe, where it is known by the loss of all its loved ones. This is not because

THE DEATH
OF A FAWN

This will I do because the woeful cry
Of life and all flesh living cometh up
Into my ears, and all my soul is full
Of pity for the sickness of this world.
—Edwin Arnold, THE LIGHT OF ASIA

W hy should I write of it? Nothing can be done to change what happened. What can be said except that it's regrettable? It's not even that uncommon an occurrence. If it hadn't cried out, I might have put the whole thing aside by now.

But it did cry out and it is that, more than anything else about the event, that refuses to be forgotten. I had never before heard a deer make any call at all. I suppose I assumed the species was mute, although I don't recall any specific thoughts about the matter. It's just that in all my life, the deer I have encountered, whether as single individuals or in herds of hundreds, were invariably voiceless. So when the fawn cried out I was utterly unprepared to hear anything at all. But of course the point of this is lost unless one knows what happened.

I'll begin with a simple recitation of the facts. Perhaps that's all that's needed. The facts may be the best anyone can do. My wife, Karen, and I were driving south on Highway 395 in eastern Oregon. It had been raining heavily, but the storm had broken up and a late afternoon sun slanted in from the west. The highway had just descended from a conifer woods and was gradually flattening out into the sagebrush and grass country of the Great Basin. Karen and I both saw the sign indicating a deer crossing and had noted to each other that we should stay alert. The highway climbed a little rise and then descended into a shallow pocket where a small fenced enclosure set off a few acres of seeded grass from the surrounding sagebrush.

We both saw the fawn as soon as we came over the rise. We saw that it had been struck, that it was struggling to get up, that its hind legs were useless. Highway 395 is a mere ribbon of road at that point, two narrow lanes separated by a faded line of yellow paint. The stricken fawn was exactly in the center of the road, its thin legs splayed out on both sides of the lane divider. We found space to park the car and ran back to the fawn.

The fawn, terrified, tried to escape us. It stabbed at the pavement with its front legs, its little sticks of bones flailing about, its cloven hooves clattering on the asphalt, its hindquarters dragging. I could hardly bear to look at it. It was brought down like this, its little body ruined beyond recovery, and it was only a baby. I caught it up in my arms and carried it off the road and laid it on the grass. I knelt by it and held it down so that it could not struggle to rise. In the near distance, a doe paced back and forth along a fence line. Seeing her there, I knew she would not leave so long as her fawn was alive, and that as soon as Karen and I were gone she would come to the road where she stood a good chance of being struck down herself. The fawn would never again rise. It would exhaust all the life it had left trying to do so, bewildered that legs that had propelled it into a sustained run on the very day of its birth would not now carry it across a hundred yards of sage and grass to its mother.

"What are we going to do?" Karen asked. She knew, of course, as did I, but neither of us wanted to say it. "We can't leave it to suffer," I said. And then I added, "It might take days for it to die. We have to kill it." "How?" "I'm not sure," I admitted, my eyes searching the roadside for a stone heavy enough to smash a deer's skull.

Then I heard the sound of an engine and the whine of mud tires on pavement. I looked up to see a pickup truck coming over the rise where it caught the late sun, revealing the unmistakable silhouette of gun racks in the rear window. A hunter! I hailed the truck down. The driver, his eyes screwed to the road, seemed to take notice of me only at the last moment. As he slammed past us, I thought he was gone, but then the tail lights of his truck flashed and he skidded to a stop.

When he reached us, his eyes went first to the fawn. Now that I wasn't holding it down, it was struggling once more to rise. He watched it for a moment. He was chewing on the stub of an unlit cigar, and he took it from his mouth and shoved it into his shirt pocket. He touched his hand to the bill of his cap in a gesture of deference to what he saw. He asked, in a voice as soft as a whisper, "You hit it?" "No, we found it like this," I told him. "Do you have a gun?" "I don't," he said. "You wouldn't often hear me say that. We could sure use one now." He knelt by the fawn and felt its back, confirming what I already knew—its spine was broken. "I've got a pocket knife in the truck," he said. "We can cut the jugular vein."

When he got back with the knife, he opened the blade and ran his finger over it to test its sharpness. He looked at me and shrugged, pulled his cigar stub out of his pocket and stuck it back in his mouth. Then he knelt by the fawn. Karen turned away, and I heard her say, more to herself than to anyone else, "Oh, no!" and she started up the road toward our car. I said, belatedly and quite foolishly, "You better go back to the car," as if I were any better prepared than she to face what had to be done.

The hunter waited on his knees by the fawn. I got down beside him and turned the fawn's head to the side to expose its throat. From that angle, its eye stared up at us in terror and confusion. Then the hunter punched the blade into its throat.

It was then that the fawn cried out. The hunter was clearly as startled by the sound as I was. He said, "Sorry, old buddy." I needed words myself, but I hadn't any of my own at the moment, so I too said, "Sorry, old buddy." As he sawed through the flesh of the fawn's throat, he said again, "Sorry, old buddy." And I said, "Sorry, old buddy," and the fawn was mute now; the hunter's blade had sawed its voice away. Blood surged from the torn throat as the hunter and I pressed the little body against the earth. Neither of us could bear to see it try to rise again. The hunter said, "It helps to say something," and he repeated, "Sorry, old buddy." And I echoed him a third time, saying, "Sorry, old buddy."

Then the fawn's eye went blank, and its brief encounter with humans was over. The hunter and I had nothing left to say. He wiped the blade of his pocket knife on the grass and a minute later I heard the pickup start and he was gone.

But the cry of the fawn was not gone. That gaping throat and blank eye still reverberated with the sound of it and gave expression to all the suffering I have ever caused or witnessed. For the moment, my life took on such a sincerity that the pulse of it was not some emblem of being that could be timed by a wristwatch, but was being itself. This was an encounter that dashed hope of any reprieve, permitted no evasion of any sort. The fawn was dead by my own hand; its bewilderment, its terror, its innocence were facts as hard as the stones that littered the shoulder of the road. There was nothing I could look to that would soften or mitigate these realities.

The blood had begun to congeal and darken on the fawn's throat and flies were gathering on the wound. It was a corpse, as dead as anything could be. I was raised on a farm. During my childhood and early adulthood, I killed just about everything that could be eaten. My father kept a great flock of turkeys for the holiday trade, and over the course of my childhood, I killed thousands of them. There, kneeling by the roadside, I felt as if the death of the fawn bore within it all the other deaths as well. When I think of it, I am still flooded with an intractable melancholy and dismay that no momentary cheerfulness can permanently dispel. All the farm animals that died by my hand, every one of the thousands of turkeys I jammed into crates to be transported to the slaughterhouse, enter me through the cry of the fawn.

As a consequence of that single, thin cry along the shoulder of Highway 395 in eastern Oregon, I was left utterly unguarded, washed through and through with the very thing itself. I could not bear the thought of retracing the fifty yards or so that separated me from the car, turning the key in the ignition, and driving myself back into that banal and false normality where the death of a fawn is an unfortunate incident to be kept in perspective.

How can I make anyone understand this? How can I show that the death of the fawn was not a matter merely pitiable, not a matter simply of regret or guilt or remorse? How can I explain that none of the deaths of my lifetime will ever again be merely regrettable? How can I touch the tenderness in all this, convey the anguish with which the cry of the fawn pierced my heart?

It was a cry like that of Karen who, twenty days earlier, working her way down a Nevada trail so steep and eroded that it was little more than a ditch of teetering rocks, caught the toe of her boot and fell. With the leading foot wedged and the following foot trapped behind the first, her body tilted and, arching outward and down, slammed full length into the rocks with nothing but the ineffectual failure of one thin arm to break the fall. She lay for a long instant, blood running from her mouth and from a hand split upon some sharp edge. Her eyes swam up from their sudden bed of stones like the eyes of one drowning beneath the waters of her own life's current. She saw from that sunken and solitary depth how the canyon walls rose into the blue summer sky, and she said, through bubbles of blood forming at her lips, "I've done it now." She sat in the trail trying to comprehend what had happened to her while I bound her split hand in moistened clothing I had stripped from myself. She probed her bloody mouth with her uninjured hand, trying to see if her teeth were still there, and she said again, "I've really done it now, haven't I?" She spoke a language of wonderment that what she had always feared might happen had, in fact, happened. Weeks later, she would remember how the canyon walls carried her to the sky from the very place of her fall.

It was a cry like that of my father who, a year before his death, aged and enfeebled, trying courageously to bear his infirmities with reserve and dignity, struggled with great effort to get his feet to the floor from the height of a hospital bed. And when he had almost succeeded, his outstretched toes just brushing the surface of the linoleum, his buttocks sliding over the edge of the mattress, I saw him wince and strain to draw himself up again. When I inquired, "What hurts you, Father?" he said, "I'm sitting on my balls, Linley." His testicles, loose with age, were squeezed painfully beneath his own weight. Too exhausted to help himself, he fumbled ineffectually with the front of his pajamas, his feet dangling above the floor. "Help me," he said, the words bleeding from him as from a wound rubbed raw.

It was a cry like that of the man who, paunchy and middle-aged, rushed up to a urinal alongside me at a rest stop on California's Interstate 5 and confided to me that he'd wet his pants. We stood there side by side, just inches between our elbows, utter strangers to each other. He didn't look at me or preface his disclosure in any way. He simply said to no one else but me because no one else was in the restroom, "I thought I was gonna make it, and I almost did, but not quite. I dribbled a little." I looked at him then, his face so near that without my reading glasses it appeared blurred. He stared straight ahead, his neck and cheeks red with embarrassment, his throat working up and down as though there was more he wanted to say or wanted to prevent himself from saying. "Can you believe they recommend diapers for my condition?" He couldn't grasp what had happened to him. It set him apart from others. He needed someone, anyone, to hear the voice of his humiliation, the anguish he felt over the betrayal wrought upon him by his body.

It was a cry like that of children anywhere when war or poverty or disaster has left them stunned and wise before their time. A cry like that of their parents who can not save them, and of all of us who have seen the young taken down while we ourselves survived. A cry like the hunter's own "Sorry, old buddy," recited like a prayer of contrition for the hard work of his hands.

We cry out from the place of our ambush, where the certainty of accident, disease, infirmity, death lies in wait for us. Our innocence is assaulted on all sides. Were we not capable of being surprised by this, we would long ago have succumbed to despair. Were we not capable of tenderness, of sorrow, we would be brutes.

If you look at a map of Oregon, you can pretty well pinpoint the exact stretch of road where the fawn was struck. You can see it in relationship to the rest of Oregon, and with a more general map, you can see its relationship to all of North America. It was, as I told you, on Highway 395, forty-one miles south of John Day and twenty-nine miles north of Burns. I tell you this because I want you to understand how Oregon spreads out from the place where the fawn died, out into Washington and Idaho and California and the Pacific Ocean. And I want you to see how none of these neighboring territories limits the extension of space, so that being, of its own nature, spreads itself across the face of the earth and beyond.

Any astronomical chart will show you that the whole universe is contiguous to the exact spot where the fawn cried out, so that absolutely everything was gathered into that cry. The cry was voiced everywhere, heard everywhere, and not just at that time, not just at 5:30 P.M. on August 25, 1997, but at all times.

You can hear it now. It is the voice of our dismay, the cry of our innocent bewilderment. It is the injury received of our ears, the wound from which our sympathy bleeds forth.

NOISE

*All things herein have
inherent great potentiality,
both function, rest, reside within.*

—Sekito Kisen, SANDOKAI

The sound of the bees reached me even with the windows closed and the refrigerator running. I was washing the breakfast dishes, water splashing into the sink, my mind intent on the task, when I became aware of the beginnings of a sound like that of a sudden wind trapped against the eaves of the house or like the first hushed vibrations raised from a cello when the bow is drawn across the strings.

I recently moved from the country to town, and here where I live there are lots of competing sounds. Noise, mostly, I call it. It is hard to distinguish one sound from the other: the sizzle of tires on the nearby freeway like fat perpetually frying; the whine of power mowers and leaf blowers and chain saws; the moaning hydraulics of trash trucks and street sweepers; the thump of stereos from passing cars; the hysterical utterings of triggered alarm systems and of the sirens of emergency vehicles; the clatter and grind of trains along the rails west of town, their horns wailing at the crossings; the whine of the helicopter lifting from the roof of Enloe Hospital; dogs barking from the confinement of backyards; the voices of humans, their shouts, laughter, fragments of conversation. Sometimes I am so drowned in the noise of others that the sound of own life is rendered mute. I can't hear myself. I cease to have any aural existence whatsoever.

That's the way it was the morning I stood at the sink washing the breakfast dishes. So it was all the more surprising that I heard the bees because they had to penetrate the peculiarly dulling sound that noise makes. But the bees reached me with a sound that separated itself from the rest and insisted on being heard. I shut the faucet off. Listened. Wondered. I went to the door and pulled it open, whereupon the sound I was hearing was suddenly and greatly amplified. On the back porch, it took me a minute to realize that the space above my head was alive with a great swarm of bees.

A catalpa tree overhangs my back yard. Its heart-shaped leaves, some as large as the spread of two hands, arch over a concave of their own making, like the hollow of a parachute blown open by the force of its descent. The sun overhead lights up the catalpa leaves so that their undersides show translucent, shimmering greenly with a radiance that seems self-originating. It was here that I discovered the bees—hundreds of them—crisscrossing, in streaks of random intricacy, the hollow beneath the tree, their bodies glowing like tiny golden satellites flung against a firmament of luminous leaves. The bees had reached me with the sound of light. They were gathering me into the song the sun sings, into the source of my own song.

We cannot fabricate our own being, we can only receive it. To be alive means receiving ourselves, not once only, but ever, and not from our own hand, but always from the hand of something other, existing as ourselves only through the agency of what is not ourselves. To be means to be in relationship. Our eyes, ears, tongues, our whole bodies are the gates of our being, the hinges upon which the mind swings. It is not so much that we take hold of life by going out through these gates as that life takes hold of us by coming in. We enter ourselves in this manner.

A sound like that of the bees has this power of confirmation, of gathering us into the moment of our mutually being there. This gathering is an act of mind. It is reciprocal: mind recognizing the presence of mind, mind receiving mind. In what we call noise, the mind fails to discern the presence of itself. Noise measures the demise of mind.

Noise is frequently annoying, but it is not annoyance that defines it as such. The crows in my neighborhood are feeding their young these days and they sometimes persist in their raucous cawing from dawn to dark. My neighbor, on his way to work the other morning, couldn't contain his annoyance any longer. He stood under the tree in his front yard looking up into its branches and ordered the crows to "Shut up!" The sound of a crow shares with the sound of a leaf blower the capacity to be annoying, but the sound of a crow arises from the common well of silence; it possesses its own life, lives in itself, and is thus capable of calling the mind into relationship. The sound of a leaf blower is the consequence of mechanical contrivance. It does not live in itself, and it cannot call us into relationship. We cannot impart to the voice of a machine the living silence from which our own voice has come. It is this deficiency in being, and thus in silence, that defines a sound as noise. In noise all the spaces are crammed, allowing for no entry.

It is through the agency of silence that sound is heard. Our human voices, in speech or song, in laughter or weeping, in sigh or gasp or groan, would be incomprehensible without this attendant silence. The dawn song of a meadowlark, the rasp of a cricket under the darkening hedge, the notes of a violin concerto, the chime of a doorbell, the crunch of footsteps on a graveled path would each be only noise except that its silence be as audible as its sound.

This silence, which is both space and pause, is inherent in all beings. Our human body manifests it as pulse, the pause between heartbeats, the point of rest between the exhalation and inhalation of breath. Such silence resides in the very tissues of which we are formed: in the spaces separating the material components of our cells, in the structured vacancy that allows for the dance of molecules, in the infinitesimal vastness of the atom, where electrons orbit the charged nucleus, in the furthest descent into the microbeing of our existence where matter virtually dissolves into space, and silence is all that is left.

The mind too is characterized by space and pause. Our perceptions arise as intervals of motion within a ground of stillness. Such stillness is integral to all thought and makes consciousness itself possible. In December 1995, I underwent spinal surgery, and for five hours I lay unconscious.

When consciousness returned, it came to me first as sound. I heard someone ask, "How're you doing, Mr. Jensen? The surgery went fine." Then, through the haze, the face of a woman took shape, tufts of red hair showing at the edges of her nurse's cap, freckles, the eyes coming clear, as green as the gown she wore. "Dr. Fleming will be in to see you soon. The surgery went just fine," she repeated. I could not have expressed then what I know how to say now: that the anesthesia that had temporarily taken away the motion of my mind had also taken its stillness; that with the return of sound, silence was returned to me as well. It gathered me into the moment; it spoke from each of us to the other, her silence and mine.

I speak of this incident because we are all exposed, chronically and fatally, to the numbing assault of noise. Everywhere we go, the incessant noise of our machinery wears away at the life-sustaining stillness of our natural minds. It invades even our speech where the dulling monologue of television, allowing for no response, closes all gaps, shuts tight all spaces, squeezes out all stillness, so that we are put to sleep long before bedtime. In such an environment, either we awaken or we ourselves become machines.

The silence within us seeks the silence without; the silence within *is* the silence without. In this way I am gathered into the sound of the bees. The hum of their tiny wings holds deepest converse with the spaces between things, the silent interstices of the mind. The being that arises from this silence arises every moment and is common to all, at once singular and universal, neither one nor many, forming itself out of its own absence.

GOING BEYOND

*"I soften the edges of intent
that I not reside
within the fixed and narrowed
center of my will."*

THE SONG
NOT HEARD

I sustained a hearing loss from a blow to the head when I was a boy, so I can never be the accomplished birder that at times I wish I could be. You know, the one who gets out of the car, and before he has advanced a dozen steps along the birding route, has already identified by voice more species that the rest of us will be able to locate in an hour of concentrated search. But whatever public ambitions I may have had, I have always known that the greater loss, the purely private loss, was that I would never hear clearly the songs of many birds. But something happened recently to show me how such losses are redeemed.

A few months ago I was birding a field of mixed sage and grass when a Brewer's sparrow popped up on a sage clump so near to where I stood that I had no need of binoculars to see even the most subtle details. I held motionless, and the Brewer's sparrow either accepted my presence or did not sense me at all. A light wind was up and the sound of it rustled through the sage. The little bird swayed on its perch.

Then the sparrow stretched its head and neck forward and up, its little bill opened, its throat pulsed in and out, and a tiny tremor ran through its whole body, the bill itself vibrating delicately for an instant before it closed in repose. This was repeated several times: the outward inclination, the parting bill, the throat working, the rising shiver, then all of it pulled back in again to perfect containment—a rhythm I received like the expansion and contraction of my own heart.

I heard not a note of the bird's song, only the wind that flowed around us and between us and swayed this little creature on its perch where, from my point of "disadvantage," it seemed to throw its very body into every rising of song. I saw the living anatomy, the physiology of the bird's call. I saw that sound and note, could I have heard them, were only the extension, the outermost extremity of pulsing blood and feathers, breath, flesh, and brittle bone.

To see like this is much like losing the sound portion of a TV program, where the framed image suddenly lapses into silence that communicates a reality unavailable when sound is present. The figures on the screen move about in mute animation, their faces and bodies telling you something you could not otherwise have "heard."

At length, I moved and the Brewer's sparrow flew away. I saw then that the clump of sage where the little bird had sung its song was itself singing in the wind.

SEEING

To carry yourself forward and
experience myriad
things is delusion.
That myriad things come forth
and experience themselves is awakening.
—Great Master Dogen, GENJO KOAN

Mother was seated at the kitchen table. I was seated beside her, near enough to touch her if I were to reach out. It was the second day of my visit. Father, who always treated me as a guest upon first arrival, was settling once more into his customary routine and had gone outdoors to sweep leaves off the drive. Mother took advantage of his absence to talk to me about a book she had been reading and some ideas in which Father had little interest.

Her face was turned from me toward a window that opened on the back yard so that as she talked, I watched her in profile. The sun from the window lit up her face and hair. She was absorbed in what she was saying, punctuating her words with crisp little bobbings of her head and emphatic hand gestures. I recall that she asked my opinion on something, the content of which I have long forgotten or never knew, because it was exactly then that I realized I was seeing my mother as if I had never seen her before.

Her hair, gray then in her late sixties, the wrinkles radiating from the corners of her eyes and around her mouth, her lips, thinner than they once were, pressed together in the pauses between sentences, the sharp insistence of her gaze when she turned to inquire for my response—nothing about any of this was new to me. Yet for the moment these features seemed divested of all my forty-four years' experience of her. I needed to recite to myself that this woman was Lucy Beatrice Jensen, and that she was my sixty-six-year-old mother whom I knew to be, in every detail, exactly the person that sat opposite me.

She was suddenly still, as though holding her breath in anticipation of what was to come. The eyes behind the lenses of her glasses were questions. I took her hand, holding it as if it were something I had just found. Mother said, "Yes, I'm growing old." I understood that she referred to the chloasma that had appeared on the backs of her hands. But that was not it; I had long been aware of such changes. How could I explain to her or to myself that in all her familiarity, she was utterly new to me at that moment?

My mother, eighty-six now, still lives. I have known her for sixty-four of those years. Yet this tiny episode of twenty years ago, little more than a single minute, persists. It has a reality that refuses to be ignored. It resists all my ideas of it. So for most of the twenty years since Mother and I sat down to talk, that brief moment with her at the kitchen table has stuck in my mind like a buried splinter I can't get rid of. But something happened recently that bears upon this event and uncovers its working in all its original force and detail.

I am a Soto Zen Buddhist and I practice Zen meditation. For some years now I have traveled once or twice a year to a Soto monastery near Mount Shasta, California, for periods of intensive training in this practice. Two months ago, on the twenty-first of August, at four in the afternoon, I was in residence at this monastery. Except for what happened then, I would not now be writing these words. I was seated in the meditation hall. Reverend Kodo, the meditation monitor, had set the incense burning and lit the candle. Perhaps half an hour had elapsed since she had sounded the gong to begin meditation. I was among twenty or so lay Buddhists spaced around the perimeter of the room sitting cross-legged and facing the wall, which is our custom. A stillness had settled on the room.

Out of that stillness, there came to mind a line from a Soto scripture we recite daily at the monastery: "The absolute upright holds, as it is, many phenomena within its own delicate balance." Whatever sense the line might hold for me, it came to me then less like a thought than like a living presence. It moved within and straightened me by some intent other than my own. It rose into my eyes, where the afternoon sun leaking through the pines outside the windows threw shifting patterns on the wall before me. It was as if Catherine, the Soto monk who first taught me meditation posture, had reached me across the intervening years to make one last adjustment, or as if Reverend Kodo herself had arisen from her own meditation nearby and, putting her knowing hands to the task, had gently coaxed my body into the "absolute upright."

I did not yet know the extent of what had happened, but I began to discover it as soon as I arose from meditation. The Buddha statue reflecting the flame of the altar candle, the other trainees passing along the north windows toward the door, Reverend Kodo barefoot in her purple robe waiting to close the meditation hall, all pressed themselves upon me with a sudden immediacy over which I had no control. I turned to go, passing the windows where the light spilled into my eyes.

Twenty years collapsed into an instant; once again, my mother at the kitchen table, the sun in her face, the sound of her morning talk echoing in the emptying meditation hall. Outside, I met Reverend Seikai on the garden path. He too seemed altered in some way I could not fathom. The garden itself, the rows of tomatoes and squash and beans, the greenhouse windows stained with moss, the compost bins, the monks' enclosure beyond the garden, the distant flanks of Mount Shasta, all these changed in some way I simply could not blink off. But changed how? Changed so fully into themselves that I did not know them from before.

The town of Chico lies in the northern extremity of California's Central Valley. I live in an area of this town locally referred to as "the avenues." It is a neighborhood of older houses and mature trees that have pushed up the sidewalks and overarched the streets. Adjacent to the avenues is a cemetery with wide lawns, ancient valley oaks, and a few maples whose fallen leaves paint the ground in the shortening days of late October and November. It is a wonderful place to walk and I do, at least once a day, for both the exercise and the pleasure it brings me.

It was on one of these walks, after my return from the monastery, that I realized my line of sight had shifted upward. This was the case whatever I happened to be doing: walking or listening to a friend or drinking a cup of coffee or meditating. Naturally I still looked downward to do things like stepping off curbs or washing dishes, but in their neutral position my eyes looked out on a dead level. On the surface this might seem trivial, a postural change so minor that the closest of friends would be unlikely to notice. But our eyes are situated at the vertex of an angle where even the finest adjustment has profound consequences as the line of the angle extends into the distance. Thus the whole of my visual perspective was altered.

For one thing, there was more for my eyes to deal with. Before, when I tended to look downward, I effectively reduced the complexity of what I saw. My eyes took in objects nearer at hand, and there were fewer of them. All I had to cope with was the hundred feet of pathway in front of me and perhaps some lawn and gravestones on either side, a few bushes with sparrows flying in and out.

But now, looking out on a level, I had to contend with every earthly thing between me and the horizon. My peripheral vision expanded as well so that my eyes were flooded from the edges with more images than I could recognize: not only the blossoming myrtle tree, but the scrub jay beneath the myrtle as well, the sprinkler in the foreground splashing water on the gravestones, the oak with its limb broken away, a squirrel motionless on an elm trunk, leaves scattering on the wind, children running on the far lawn of Chico Junior High, a vapor trail spread on the sky, an endless, momentary multiplication of interstices jammed with objects of sight, a limitless periphery of visual information remaining everlastingly beyond the power of focus.

I had entered an enlarged and uncertain visual universe where I was seeing more than I could ever consciously recognize. Yet even the most marginal objects came to me with the same living insistence that had begun at the monastery. Not being used to this, my eyes themselves seemed to falter, undecided about what to look at.

How is it that it has taken me sixty-four years to discover that the present moment is swifter than thought? My body, in its intrinsic and native power of sight, has always understood this. It reads life directly and is teaching me now to do so as well. It has loosened my hold on things that they might move, as they must, along the sequence of the moment. It has shown me that this sycamore rooted to the banks of Chico Creek on this blustery afternoon in mid-October cannot be held in place beyond the instant of my seeing it here any more than its yellowing leaves can be held from their fall to earth. I know now that the only sycamore I can hold on to has its roots sunk nowhere but in my thoughts of it. If I try to hold on to Reverend Seikai in this way he will appear entirely familiar, for the one I meet on the garden path will be nothing but an idea of my own making. If for even a second this idea of him drops away, I bring to sight what I could not see before: Reverend Seikai, exactly himself, in the instant of his passing there.

I have not risked seeing the world as it actually is. My

eyes have snatched at things, picked and sorted them, until there was little left to see but an arbitrary arrangement of my own thoughts. Between classes at Chico State University, students by the hundreds crisscross the quad on their way to various destinations. Watching them, I have discovered that most of them look down, their eyes controlling the short patch of ground into which they forever walk. Those who look up stare ahead with such singleness of purpose that I marvel they do not run into each other. Only a few have eyes that risk the present moment. These few know one another on sight, a circumstance acknowledged in glances of mutual recognition.

In Soto Zen Buddhism, we are taught to meditate with our eyes open. We sit facing a wall, and we are instructed not to stare at the wall but to maintain a gentle focus. I never understood what this gentle focus was or how it was achieved. I would sometimes lower my eyelids until the wall became a kind of blur, but I knew that was not the intended outcome. I had never been clear about what I was supposed to do with my eyes. I know now that I was not supposed to do anything with them at all. To see with a gentle focus means to limit doing and entrust my eyes to the periphery where seeing is done by itself. I soften the edges of intent that I not reside within the fixed and narrowed center of my will. The absolute upright holds by inclusion: it lets everything in. Its eye forever opens on the fullness of itself, where edges join the center and sight receives things as they are.

Five hundred miles south of Chico, my mother lives alone now that Father has died. I will visit her soon and I

THE MIND OF
THE MOUNTAIN

What I have to say about Mount Shasta has its beginnings in Room 607 of Western Medical Hospital in Tustin, California. It was there in the final seconds of my father's life that I first glimpsed the mind of the mountain.

At half past noon on the eighth of December 1993, I sat alone at my father's bedside as I had done for the seven preceding days. He lay on his side, his body clenched round itself so that his legs were drawn up nearly to his chest. His eyes were tightly shut as if by force of some conscious intent. His eyelids twitched and from time to time would raise just the merest bit so that for an instant he would seem to squint into the pillow or perhaps the curtain where it was drawn round to divide the room. His arms, exposed outside the bedding, were stained purple with errant blood leaked from wasted veins.

At times his hands repeatedly and pointlessly clutched the sheets or each other or nothing at all that I could discern. I worried terribly about this. "What is it, Father? What do you want?" I would reach in with my own hands, and he would grasp at them with the same erratic lack of pattern with which he grasped at the blanket or anything else. In the end I couldn't understand what these motions meant. I found it increasingly difficult to separate which of the two of us was reaching out from the bed and which was reaching in, who was dying and who was watching, who was going, who staying. I felt unbearably bounded and imprisoned, as if I too were clamped tight behind my father's shut lids.

All this was to change. Shortly before one o'clock on the afternoon of the eighth, Father opened his eyes, alert and full, as he had not done since he had collapsed on his bedroom floor seven days before. He seemed to be seeing something that I did not see. He reached out toward whatever it was, his withered arms straining, an IV tube trailing from a vein in his wrist. And he spoke to something unknown to me, his lips forming the syllables of voiceless words.

"Father?" I questioned. He responded not at all. I passed my hand before his eyes. Nothing. I bent over until my face intersected exactly his line of sight, my own eyes looking directly into his, just inches between us. The eyes that met my own were brightly alive; yet I saw then that I did not exist for him. His mind had simply looked the room away so that the intervention of a son's eyes or the curtain drawn round his bed or the walls of room 607 itself were swept aside like so much dust before a broom. It was as if he had canceled all dimension and set aside even the least of boundaries so that the two of us no longer occupied a space fixed firmly by the mind. I felt as though I had been ripped out of all confines and flung like a night wind somewhere on the dark side of the planet.

And then I saw the living presence in my father's eyes yield to absence, and I heard the last breath of his long life rattle out from collapsing lungs. The room was ordinary again, the bed squared to the wall, the window with blinds shut against the noonday glare, the curtain on its ceiling track drawn across a dead man's remains. The nurses, alerted by the monitor, descended on me to confirm that, indeed, my father had no pulse. Yet something lingered there of a spaciousness beyond the power of any design or procedure to contain.

In the weeks following my father's death, I lived diminished. The ordinary events of life were as confining to me as the lowered coffin that held my father's remains. So in early March when a small group of us traveled to the Lower Klamath Basin to see the wintering waterfowl, I was grateful for the diversion. I rode northward in the back seat of a friend's vehicle confined between two others who had the windows and who commented from time to time on the country we were passing through. I could see little of it from where I sat. I made small talk there in the back seat and was pointedly congenial. I thought that perhaps in the morning I could better match my feelings to my words.

The morning was cold. The wind swept across the waters of the Lower Klamath Refuge, insinuating itself into whatever gaps remained around our throats or the backs of our necks or our sleeve ends or wherever our woolens did not quite meet. I had never seen the basin before, and when we made our first stop and I had unloaded myself from the car and actually stepped out into the open, I saw that it was a place of great space and light and weather. The wild marsh and grasslands of the basin spread out in all directions, carrying my eye to the very curve of the earth's horizon. Nothing contrived was adequate to tame the dimensions of the place, certainly not the sparse network of pavement nor the car we huddled in when the wind got too much for us, nor any gathering of cars and birders that might converge on a sighting, nor the logical symmetry of the visitor's center at Tule Lake. Everything was taken up in reference to that greater space.

Above all this stood the silent white pyramid of Mount Shasta. In the austerity of the basin where the absolute upright of the mountain was anchored to the most uncompromising flatness, I saw how each derived its being from the other, the mountain taking source from the plain, the plain from the mountain. From where I stood in the basin below, I came to understand that the mind could rise to the mountain only if it began its journey from the plain; that within all our going up there lives as well our going down. On the marsh, a flock of swans floated in the inverted image of the mountain. For the moment I knew it was not possible to float if it was not also possible to sink, a truth that may be hard to acknowledge when the waters are closing over one's head. Yet the mountain held me suspended that day wherever I went.

A bald eagle pushed off from its perch and soared through a melee of thousands of scrabbling pintails, the whole event etched against the white flanks of the great mountain. Ten thousand snow and Ross geese, whose whiteness stood out starkly against the brown winter grass, rose into delicate obscurity against the whiteness of the mountain, their black wing tips disembodied, stroking white on white. A pair of mating red-tailed hawks in courtship flight soared in dark silhouette across the face of the mountain and, dropping down, led my eyes to where a stack of twigs and grass, layered round and concave to a precise purpose, clung to a cliff face high above Tule Lake. All those lives, like the wind flowing over the basin, were borne forward with the same selfless absorption with which the mountain rose in fire ages ago and with which it now drinks the winter snows.

Whatever swam the basin waters that day or flew its skies or sank roots in mud or layered twigs on cliff faces or huddled in heated cars was secured within the vast scale of the basin and the long reach of the mountain that guarded it. The smallest gesture, the most inconsequential thought, was given its place in that greater order. The stricken father uncurling within my mind brought me to wonder if it was this that his dying eyes had opened upon.

Later that same month I traveled north again to join fellow Buddhists in a week of meditation at Shasta Abbey, a Zen Buddhist monastery a few miles north of the town of Mount Shasta. On the evening of my arrival, the resident monks and we lay Buddhists gathered in the dining hall for our evening meal. As is our custom, we ate in silence. Though there were over sixty of us, the only sounds were those of utensils or dishes or the occasional sliding of a chair across the wooden floor. As is also our custom, we clasped the palms of our hands together before our faces and bowed to receive each item of food or drink as it was passed to us along the length of the table. By chance, I was seated facing a long bank of windows that opened toward the north. Preoccupied as I was with the first affairs of the meal, this fact had not yet registered on me.

But when the first dish reached me and I had bowed to receive it, I raised my head to see that there, overshadowing the north windows of the dining hall where I sat and overshadowing the whole of the monastery and the little town of Shasta itself, was the great upward sweep of the mountain converging to a summit flushed crimson in the late evening sun. And each time I bowed to receive food, it was as if I bowed to receive the mountain as well.

The food comes and is passed on. The mountain comes and is passed on. In this way we receive our lives, and in this way we relinquish them as well, not once only, but again and again in every moment of our being. Our very minds are given to us in the exact instant of their going.

The mind of the mountain is none other than our own mind. There is nothing mystical in this, nothing at odds with the ordinary. We would all see this is so, could we but call ourselves fully into view. In the monks' enclosure beyond the dining hall hangs the temple bell. It waits to be struck that it may call forth itself. In her quarters off the enclosure, the abbess takes her meal alone, her legs paralyzed by the ravages of diabetes. "I am dying from the bottom up," she once declared to the monks. Thus, the abbess yields herself up to fact.

Season after season, the mountain called Shasta is wearing down to an inevitable symmetry of its own becoming. Yet, under the thrust of the shouldering oceanic plate, the whole mass of the mountain lifts so that it forms itself by ever rising into its own going down. The abbess too is wearing away into exactly what she is. She rings true when struck. It is just such ordinary stuff that binds our human minds over to that of the mountain. It was this that rose to the minds of the dying father and his son in the time of the father's going down. We are shown this from every side at all times. It inheres in all we are and all we do.

Here in the dining hall when the meal is finished and the last gratitude has been given, I will gather up my table things and carry them to the washstand and wash each item with the same mindful care with which the nurses of Western Medical bathed my father's body, taking up one hand at a time to wash between his fingers. When all is clean, I will stack the bowl on the plate and the cup in the bowl. I will lay the knife, fork, and spoon on the plate alongside the bowl. I will drape the white napkin over the stacked items with the name tag showing. I will put these things in the cupboard on the dining hall porch and join the others for evening meditation.